T0361411

Lone Twin

Social Fictions Series

Series Editor

Patricia Leavy (*USA*)

International Editorial Advisory Board

Carl Bagley (*University of Durham, UK*)
Anna Banks (*University of Idaho, USA*)
Carolyn Ellis (*University of South Florida, USA*)
Rita Irwin (*University of British Columbia, Canada*)
J. Gary Knowles (*University of Toronto, Canada*)
Laurel Richardson (*The Ohio State University (Emerita), USA*)

VOLUME 30

Lone Twin

A True Story of Loss and Found

By

Laurel Richardson

BRILL

SENSE

LEIDEN | BOSTON

Cover illustration: "Kindergarten," qrt quilt created by Laurel Richardson in self-portrait workshop of Sue Benner, fiber artist. Photograph by Josh Walum.

All chapters in this book have undergone peer review.

The Library of Congress Cataloging-in-Publication Data is available online at http://catalog.loc.gov

ISSN 2542-8799
ISBN 978-90-04-41134-0 (paperback)
ISBN 978-90-04-41135-7 (hardback)
ISBN 978-90-04-41136-4 (e-book)

This book is printed on acid-free paper and produced in a sustainable manner.

ADVANCE PRAISE FOR
LONE TWIN

"I read everything that Laurel Richardson writes. *Lone Twin: A True Story* is in my mind her best. Laurel invites us into her friendships and family life as she moves through stories of the role 'twins'—the concept and the experience—have had in her life. The writing is extraordinary— the storytelling and literary turn of phrase; the particular detail that takes your breath, unfolding a video of experience in front of you, hers and then yours; sensuous descriptions that have you reading them over and over, simply because you can't bear to leave them behind. This book takes you in and out of life, love, attachment, and loss. Laurel's work is historical, sociological, existential, literary, and above all a well-told story that will grab your heart and soul, inviting you too to ask questions of your life, and possibly construct and live a new story. Her story lingers with me now and I am mesmerized with how I might rewrite and redeem myself and my family, as Laurel has done."
Carolyn Ellis, Distinguished University Professor Emerita, Department of Communications, University of South Florida

"I read it straight away—indeed I couldn't put it down—and didn't. I found it a complete page-turner."
Juliet Mitchell, Professor of Psychoanalysis and Gender Studies at the University of Cambridge, and Emeritus Fellow of Jesus College

"Laurel Richardson has been a master storyteller of personal events, families, and relationships for her entire career. But what do you do with those stories when a revelation late in life turns all those events and relationships upside down? In *Lone Twin*, Richardson's rewrite of her life enriched by this new knowledge—including brilliant stories of her twinning with friends and family—is both emotionally revelatory and a reader's delight."
Mitch Allen, University of California–Berkeley

"This time renowned American writer and sociologist Laurel Richardson has written a thriller that builds towards a most unexpected ending. In her unique and brilliant style, she probes her life and family history to reveal much about friendship and family secrets."
Julie White, Associate Professor and Principal Research Fellow, Victoria University, Melbourne

"Laurel Richardson at her most brilliant—my generation's best writer. Family, another word for pain, and a measure of what we have lost and then re-gained; a vision of what might have been—poetic, haunting, mesmerizing."
Norman Denzin, Distinguished Professor of Communications, College of Communications Scholar, and Research Professor of Communications, Sociology, and Humanities at the University of Illinois, Urbana-Champaign

"*Lone Twin* is a book about human connection, its joys and its weight that pulls on a life, sometimes without one knowing why. It reads like a sociological case study, a memoir, a family history, and an intriguing mystery, but most of all, as an object lesson of what matters in our personal lives. From the beginning, readers will find themselves caught up in this beautifully rendered world. By the book's end, they will feel privileged to have met the people who populate this world and will be carried to the entanglements of their own relationships."
Ronald J. Pelias, Emeritus Professor, Southern Illinois University

"*Lone Twin* is a compelling book: complex, enchanting, poignant, sharp, funny, and much, much more. Richardson takes the reader on an extraordinary, surprising journey into her life-long twin-like experiences. The book's stories of friendships, perhaps-friendships and family relationships are each shot through with compassion, fearlessness, and Richardson's customary eye for detail, ear for dialogue, and sense of place (in particular the Chicago of her childhood). We feel Richardson, those others who people her book, and the places they inhabit, in the room with us, alive and close. In turn, this immediacy animates the questions of secrecy, love, loss, fear, hope, and mystery

their stories engage with. I read 'Lone Twin' in two sittings: the first took me to the final chapter. I stopped at that point so I could savour the final chapter the next day. I didn't want the book to end."
Jonathan Wyatt, Professor of Qualitative Inquiry, University of Edinburgh

"I love this book so much. I started reading it yesterday morning and read all day. In this beautiful, deeply moving collection of coming-of-age stories, Laurel Richardson reflects on the enchantment of twins, and the human need to intertwine in meaningful relationships. She captures the desire for connection in haunting prose and an unflinching narrative. Richardson is known for her writing: *Lone Twin* is her best writing ever."
Jessica Smartt Gullion, PhD, Associate Professor of Sociology, Texas Woman's University and author of *Diffractive Ethnography: Social Sciences and the Ontological Turn* and *Writing Ethnography*

"Laurel Richardson has outdone herself. *Lone Twins* is a riveting journey of how the physical, mental, and emotional hurts and longings of childhood and our (mis)connections with others mold our desires and sense of self. Richardson asks the 'what if' questions about life, love, and connection with unflinching honesty: What if you found a twin in a friend, a neighbor, or peer? What if you could talk to them with just eye blinks of understanding? What if you could find a twinned connection with others and find your own strength by working through questions of identity, girl rage, loneliness, and competition? What happens to that connection when the inevitable difficulties of life and loss intervene? I will be using this book in my relational and gender communication classes."
Sandra L. Faulkner, author of *Poetic Inquiry: Method, Craft, and Practice* (Routledge)

"I've always admired and enjoyed Laurel Richardson's lyrical writing and her latest work is no exception. She has quite a story to tell and she tells it deftly. This is a captivating compelling memoir. This is a story of secrets, intuition, clues, a complex family, and a final truth

on a deathbed. On the way to the truth we have a captivating story of a family, a girl/woman who is immensely talented, intuitive, and inquisitive who finally gets answers to long-concealed information. Her story is spellbinding and continues to linger with me."
Susan Knox, writer of short stories, essays, and creative nonfictions

"A woman who was once called little Miss Perfect reflects on childhood friendships, torturous and intimate, and the cruelties of her siblings and parents. She digs even deeper in search of a part of herself that is missing. If you have ever felt an original loss, you will want to follow the journey of this woman named Laurel, as imperfect as you and as I, as she does the brave, inspiring work of redemption."
Maggie Kast, fiction and creative non-fiction author of *The Crack between the Worlds, A Free, Unsullied Land, Side by Side and Never Face to Face: A Novella and Stories* (Orison Books, forthcoming)

"In this intimate memoir, Laurel Richardson provides insight into the importance of uncovering family secrets and recovering lost pieces of ourselves even when it seems too late to matter. *Lone Twin* explores the gaps and mysteries in our lives that hover in our dreams and on the edge of consciousness until they are confronted and resolved."
Erica Scurr, M.F.A., creative non-fiction

"Simply put, I found *Lone Twin* to be riveting. It's a stunner for book-clubs, too! Laurel's personal family story, complete with humor, pathos, drama, secrets and rituals, evoked my own family stories. I was moved by the raw honesty of her words, always clear, often poetic. As a psychologist/psychotherapist for 45 years, I would encourage clinicians at all levels to read Laurel's book. Moreover, I believe that clients, young and old, will find value in the book. We are reminded that family secrets impact everyone in the constellation. Once revealed, we can better make the journey to wholeness."
Ellyn Geller, Psychotherapist, Princeton, NJ

Life can only be understood backwards;
but it must be lived forwards.

Søren Kierkegaard

CONTENTS

PREFACE

On her death bed, my sister whispered to me a family secret. Those whispered words gave me the clues I needed to make sense of my life: Why do I feel so *alone?* Why do I feel that "something is missing"? Why do I question my right to be alive?

Lone Twin: A True Story of Loss and Found answers those questions. It is a story of a search for identity, wholeness, and forgiveness. I write of my relationships with a suicidal poet, a Swedish fencer, a budding scientist, a Puerto Rican family, a wealthy Jewish family, a Mafia family, and my famous cousin. And, I write of the neglect and abuse I experienced within my Russian Jewish and Irish Catholic family.

The story takes place in mid-to-late Twentieth Century American cities—Chicago, New York, and Los Angeles. During this time period, recovery from the Great Depression began followed by World War II's Holocaust, the Cold War, and the ossification of educational, economic, and legal institutions. Countering these, the 1950's and 1960's generate social movements—second wave feminism, civil rights and gay rights, the anti-war movement and environmentalism. The end of the century witnessed the rise of popular culture and the rise of high-rises. These historical realities are not simply backdrops in *Lone Twin*, they structured the paths available to the people living then just as people today are shaped by paths available to them. This kind of research and writing is known as *critical autoethnography.*

My father trained me from preschool on to remember in exacting detail whatever I heard or saw. Because the stories in this book come from my remembered experiences, they are true. To put the stories in their historical contexts, I did research. All the historical facts (even the horrid ones) are true. But, because I believe that the "truest story" is one that resonates emotionally with the reader, I have employed literary techniques such as doubling, dialogue, and imagery to tell the stories: I deliberately blur the lines between *fiction* and *non-fiction.*

This kind of writing is known variously as *creative non-fiction*, *social fiction*, or *life-writing*.

***

I wanted *Lone Twin* to illuminate a period of social history in America, and for readers to find it relevant to contemporary social issues, inside and beyond the borders of America. To accomplish this goal, I weave together multiple themes and highlight, here, four central ones.

NAMES: Who has the power to name whom and with what consequences? Everyone's name in this book has been deliberately chosen based on ethical, sociological, and literary concerns. I use the given names of my family members. All other names have been changed but in my re-naming I have preserved everyone's ethnic/ religious background. Cultural and religious diversity and historical accuracy are retained.

I begin *Lone Twin* with two words: "I'm Laurel." Within the book's pages, I am addressed by different names—Laurel, Laurie, Layah, Sister, Little Miss Perfect. Each name communicates a particular kind of *relationship* and tells the reader where I am in time and space and with whom I am communicating. I end with a redemption story about my name, *Laurel*. Literally, and literarily, I have "found myself."

FRIENDSHIP: Friendships are voluntary, intimate, and non-exclusive. Because they are not mandated, legalized, or protected, *friendship* interests sociologists. Who is friends with whom? What do friendship patterns tell us about the openness of a society? Do friendships replace dysfunctional family ties? And, of course, how do friends influence each other's beliefs and behaviors, provide emotional support, and play crucial roles in people's lives? In *Lone Twin*, Laurel is a "serial BFF." In seeking a best friend, she moves across social classes, religions, and ethnicities, and becomes attached to girls with differing abilities, strengths, and needs. She lives *intersectionality*.

SECRECY: The sociologist Georg Simmel noted that although all social life depends on communication, people tend to move toward artifice, concealment and lying. Sometimes people lie to protect their best interests or to aggrandize themselves or to have a little fun, or from forgetfulness. But sometimes people lie to protect *others* because they think the truth is too dangerous or hurtful to be told. Different people in *Lone Twin* fabricate stories, equivocate, and conceal truths. Why? With what consequences?

INEQUALITY: "You would change the world so you and your kind would have a better deal" was scrawled across one of my papers by a high-school teacher. I was mortified, ashamed, and embarrassed. *Who is my kind?* I wondered. *Smart girls? Half-Jewish people? Half-Irish people? Last born children?* I remember nothing about this teacher other than his degrading comment. But he has had a life-long impact on me. What is wrong with people wanting a better life for themselves and their "kind," people with whom they identify? What inequalities can be contested and changed? How can privileged people use those privileges to reduce inequality?

Lone Twin is a weaving of many themes that are still relevant. For example, the *media*—then as now—plays a major role in seeking, or prohibiting, *legal and social justice. White, upper-middle class* people continue to have *privileges.* Tensions between *religious communities* persist. *Medical* intervention and medical progress is not always "good." *Death, drugs, suicide, cancer. Children* are not always safe in their homes. Roles of *fathers. Single mothers. Ethnic pride. Beauty.*

And always and forever—*unanticipated consequences.*

***

If I knew everything I felt and thought, I could not write. I write *for discovery*, to find out what I feel and think. That is my practice and has been for decades. I had no idea, though, that writing *Lone Twin: A True Story of Loss and Found* would bring me to interior places that frighten me.

I invite the readers of *Lone Twin* to write for discovery as they consider their life journeys. Perhaps ask, "Who am I? How do I justify my existence?" "Why do I ___ (fill in the blank)?" And other questions that only you can ask.

ACKNOWLEDGMENTS

It is only when I sit to write Acknowledgments that I have my two greatest writing pleasures—first, seeing all together in one place all the names of the people who have supported my writing ventures, and second, thanking them, which I heartily do now. For over twenty years, the Memoir Writing Group—Bev Davis, Diana Newman, Linda Royalty, Erica Scurr, Linda Thompson, Deanne Witiak—have gently critiqued my drafts and given me a writing home. The Scriveners— Barbara Fiorini, Pat Hurley, Nancy McDonald-Kenworthy, Thom Pegan—gave me the push I needed to "write more." Elaine Ebert, Carolyn Ellis, Ellyn Geller, Nan Johnson, Maggie Kast, Susan Knox, Ben Walum, Josh Walum, Tami Walum, Akiva Walum-Roberts, Shana West, and Julie White have given precious time, wisdom, and emotional support throughout this project. Norman Denzin's presence in and leadership of The International Congress of Qualitative Inquiry (ICQI) has, in addition to his support, given me a community of like-minded people from whom my learning has been endless. Mitch Allen, Sandra Faulkner, Mark Freeman, Jessica Gullion, Ron Pelias, Juliet Miller and Jonathan Wyatt have been kind, thoughtful and generous. Patricia Leavy has been more than an editor—she has been a coach, a "fan," and a model of self-determination in the service of others. Shalen Lowell is a joy. The talented Brill | Sense staff—John Bennett, Acquisition Editor, Jolanda Karada, Production Editor, and Paul Chambers, Marketing—have done a superb job of shepherding *Lone Twin*. Ernest Lockridge read multiple drafts encouraging me to "compress," "expand," and/or "keep." Without his keen eye, gentle urging, and constancy this book would not be here. Even more, he lived with me as I emotionally relived the traumas I was writing about. Although Ernest would say, "No need to repeat yourself," I will. *Thanks.*

PART 1

WHAT

Twinhood bestows the singular oddity
of a plural identity.

Twinless Twins Support Group

ABSENCE

I'm Laurel. I lived alone once. I never want to again. I was through college, a teacher renting a basement apartment in San Francisco's Sunset District, the Pacific Ocean just outside my door, a dream come true. I should have been happy, but I wasn't. The ocean wasn't swim-worthy like Chicago's Lake Michigan; the neighborhood lacked little shops; and people were—where? Not outside, just cars, lots of indifferent cars.

Coming home after work, there is no one to greet me, ask me about my day, empathize with my leg pains. I hum a little made-up tune in the make-shift shower, put Shostakovich's Fifth on my turntable, eat a bowl of breakfast cereal, go to bed with my current novel, and soon fall asleep in the fetal position, holding a pillow. The alarm wakes me just shy of a dozen hours later. I am not lonely, a flitting-by emotional state. I am in an inexorably intolerable existential state: I am living *alone.*

***

Sixty plus years have passed since I lived in San Francisco, and during none of them have I lived alone. For the past forty-plus, I have lived with my second husband, Ernest. We dine, read, and hang-out on the sun room of our house in Worthington, Ohio. A Fung Shei expert identified the sun room as our house's "love and marriage place." Ernest is on his Kindle, I am riveted to a Roads Scholar's travel pamphlet, open on my lap.

"I don't want to travel," Ernest says. He looks piqued. He has just turned eighty.

"I know you don't," I say, hoping I sound conciliatory. "But, if •
you predeceased me, I would, in a minute, go on this around the world

trip." I point to the entry in the pamphlet. "If you weren't here, I wouldn't want to live here by myself. And, if I died on the trip, so what?"

***

I am having lunch with some long-term friends, all of us in our seventies or eighties. Three of us are married, four live alone.

"I don't ever want to live alone," I say. "I don't know how any of you do it."

"I like the freedom of not having to answer to anyone," Debbie, our host, says. She ladles her famous lentil soup into our blue Spode soup bowls.

"You build a network of support outside your house," Michelle says, crunching crackers into her soup.

"I eat what I want when I want," Mary says, slicing off a chunk of Stilton cheese. "And I don't have to clean up anyone else's shit. If there are dirty dishes in the sink, they're mine."

"I don't want to live alone, either," says Karen. She pushes in on her stomach with her folded hands. She is 78. Her 83 year old husband is failing. She is in constant grief. "I can't live alone because I need someone to talk to."

"That's not what I need," I say, surprising myself with my lack of apparent compassion for Karen. "I talk to lots of people lots of time."

"I need to be special to someone," Karen continues.

Linda gives Karen a Kleenex.

"For me," I say, "it's about fear. I would be afraid to live alone." I am dumbfounded at how I have stolen the conversation away from Karen's anticipatory grief. I try to shut up. Then, I try to remedy my rudeness by raising mundane fears that Karen might have like losing the house-key, falling and not being able to get up, thieves breaking in, water-heater breaking…

Karen nods.

…but, I know I am reciting a commonplace litany of fears older women might give for not wanting to live alone. Am I avoiding Karen's emotional state by my clichéd response? Or, avoiding my own emotional state? *Could I survive alone? Should I?*

Our conversation turns from death and dying to birth and living. One of our friends' granddaughters had trouble conceiving. She turned to IVF and has given birth to twins.

"There seems to be a lot of twins born recently," Karen says, putting the Kleenex into her purse.

"Yes," Mary agrees. "Although, you know many co-twins are terminated following the implantation of multiple embryos."

"I didn't know about that," Linda says, shaking her head.

"Hmm. We talk about abortion...but hmm," Debbie says. She twist folds her napkin.

"I am suspicious of all the twins I see," I say. I hear my voice rising and my face flushing. "I don't think of them as real twins...I think they're artificial twins...They aren't naturally twins."

"Do you think they're not human?" Linda asks. She stares at me, aghast.

"Of course they're human...they are real children but not genuine twins—*faked?*...not naturally twins—all by themselves becoming twins." My speech is getting louder and faster.

"You sure are worked up over this," Mary says.

"I am. Some damn doctor is playing God...solving a fertility problem...destroying the specialness of being a natural twin. Damn science is turning twinning into a commonplace. I don't like it."

***

When I get home, I feel contrite about my tirade but my mind is unchanged. It is too easy, now, to be a twin. *Faked* twinning? Neither twin ever has to be alone. Everywhere—double strollers.

But my judgmental statement is totally inconsistent with my behavior. I am always drawn to twins. I love them. I greet them, "Hi!" and "Hi!!" I keep e-files of photos of twins friends send me—great nephews in California, Ghanese girls in Princeton, fraternals in Colorado. I rejoice that my grandson has just become an uncle of twins. I have lovingly made each twin a quilt, one with giraffes, the other with zebras, both of them backed in yellow and white polka-dot flannel. I have a shelf of books about twins, a file drawer of articles.

I have had a life-long obsession with twins and twinning. Even in my writing I like to use the same word twice, twice preferably in the same sentence.

***

When I was two and a half, I asked Santa for two look-alike baby-dolls. When I received just one, a Dydee-Doll that could drink water and wet its diaper, I pouted and cried. Mother said that elves did not make look-alike babies and that, in any case, it was greedy of me to want two dolls when some children didn't even have one.

When I was 40, I found in a London antique store what I had spent years looking for—a pair of doll-house babies, identically dressed in white sleeping gowns and caps. They sleep, face-to-face, in a miniature bassinet on my shelf of special things.

They are neither fake nor real.

PART 2

SCHOOL GIRLS

How can a girl get on in school without her twin sister?

Twinless Twins Support Group

REAL TWINS: JOAN AND JUNE

One summer morning, Mother and I climb a flight of metal stairs to an apartment above a grocery store. A gray-haired woman invites us into the kitchen. And there they are, Joan and June, little as mice and dressed exactly alike in pink dresses embroidered with blue forget-me-nots. White lace collars frame their look-alike faces. They are real. Not dolls.

Mother is on a P.T.A. mission to find and enroll eligible children for half-day kindergarten in LeMoyne's school district which scrawls from wealthy Lake Shore Drive families through middling ones to poverty-stricken ones south of Cubs Ballpark. She enrolls Joan and June in what will be my half-day kindergarten class, too.

***

On the first day of kindergarten, I snuggle Joan under one arm and June under the other. My twins fit neatly under my armpits. *My twins.* I sit between them for the class photo. I sit between them cross-legged on the floor for music and I sit between them at our little tables, my shoes scraping the floor while theirs swing in mid-air. I let them use all my Crayolas, even the genuine gold and silver ones. I help them write their names. I protect them on the school yard fending off with shouts and fists anyone who might tease them or trample on them, which could happen because the concrete steps into our school are so deep for their short legs and sometimes they trip and fall down.

***

"Can you help June learn to add," our first-grade teacher asks me.

Mother had taken me to see Helen Keller the summer before and Helen Keller had taken my hand in hers, touching my fingers

© KONINKLIJKE BRILL NV, LEIDEN, 2019 | DOI:10.1163/9789004411364_002

and folding my fingers as she talked to me telling me I would be a very important woman some day. For my teacher to ask me to help June must mean I was already an important somebody and because of Helen Keller I had an idea of how I could help.

"June," I say, taking the thumb on her left hand in my hand, "this thumb's name is *One*."

"One," June said, wiggling her thumb.

"And this finger's name is *Two*," I say pulling on her left index finger.

"Two!" June wiggled that finger.

"Now," I said, "if we wiggle One and Two they will touch your next finger. Its name is *Three*."

"Three!"

"Yes, and One and Two together *reach* Three."

We number-name all her fingers and she learns to count and add. Joan joins in. Before long, we give other names to our fingers and finger-combinations. Soon, the three of us have a private language, a finger-code. We talk without speaking.

Into our primary grades, I walk my twins to their apartment on the way to mine. I hold their hands as we cross Addison Avenue, Joan always to my left, June always to my right, because Joan is right-handed and June is left-handed and they are most securely held by me holding their strongest little hand. I think I am the only one besides their parents who can tell them apart. June's face is a tad longer than Joan's.

Sometimes after school I climb the metal stairs with the twins to their apartment. Their gray-haired mother sets milk and cookies out for us. She looks old in her washed out wash-dress. She doesn't smile, chatter, or ask us what we learned in school. My twins' father, a retired train conductor, balding and fat around the middle, dozes in an overstuffed living room chair. Two photos are on the credenza—one of the twins as tiny babies and the other of their much older brother. He is in the Navy on a ship somewhere secret in the middle of a war.

When we are seven, my mother allows me to have over-nights at the twins' apartment. Playing in the gutter on Addison Avenue with older children I have learned how babies are made. I decide to teach my twins about it. We lie on their bed, me in the middle, with our pajama legs down around our ankles. We each take a little piece of paper, get it wet with our saliva, roll it up, and plant the "seed" in private parts. I plant a seed in each of the twins and they each plant a seed in me. Because I have two seeds, I will have twins. We keep those little pieces of paper inside until the morning. When we take the papers out, we commiserate because the papers are just soggy, smelly papers and not babies.

***

I have never written about these over-night experiences nor told anyone. They have been my secret. Why? Too intimate? No. Too suggestive of a premature sexuality? No. I think the games were an attempt to play out a deep longing in my psyche, a place that I could not consciously reach: I was not playing sex games, I was playing reproduction. I wanted twins.

***

"Where's June," I ask Joan at the beginning of fourth grade.
"A different room," Joan says.
"Why?"
"School thinks it is best to separate twins."
"That's really dumb," I say. "It makes me angry."
How could separating twins be a good thing? Says who? I can still feel the anger in my gut as I write about this. The school-system, based on who-knows-what "scientific" study had torn apart the lives of my twins, and my life with them. After that separation, I rarely see June and Joan mopes. I no longer spend much time with either of them.
In fifth grade, Joan is no longer in my classroom either. "Studies" had shown that children do best when they're tracked according to their academic abilities. Joan's academic potential was not the same as mine.

***

I have no idea what has happened to *my twins*. They stay caught in time as twin girls in sailor-girl outfits, the clothes they wore for our kindergarten class photograph. They are early characters in my life's drama. I am not proud of this. But when I allow myself to imagine them grown up I see them as happily married, neighbors to each other, loving aunts and great aunts. I imagine only the best for *my twins*.

LOOK-A-LIKES: SUSAN

I am six going on seven. My family is summering in Bluebird, our cottage at Family Camp on Geneva Lake. Bluebird has one room with four beds, a galley-kitchen with a kerosene stove and ice box, and a sleeping porch. Community toilets and showers are up the gravel path next to the pay-telephone booth.

Mr. and Mrs. Ricca and their daughter, Susan, are in camp this summer for the first time. They are in Mallard, a fancy three room cottage with indoor plumbing. It's down the gravel path nearer to the lake.

Although I call the grown-ups at Camp "Aunt' or "Uncle," even though they aren't kin, I never call Mr. and Mrs. Ricca anything other than "Missus" and "Mister." They are very rich, I think, not just because they have rented Mallard but because Susan's father has a mustache and wears a black three-piece suit, and her mother has fake eyelashes, high-heel shoes and her own car.

Mrs. Ricca treats me to the same toys and clothes she buys for Susan. She buys us look-alike sundresses with matching sunbonnets and panties. My favorite dress has heart-shaped pockets trimmed in red rick-rack; its matching hat's large heart-shaped bill hides my face; its panties have a little heart-shaped pocket, too, on a side-seam. "There," Mrs. Ricca says, "You look a-like twins."

Of course, we really don't. Susan is overweight with olive-colored skin and black short frizzy hair; I am wiry with fair skin and pigtails. But when we have matching clothes on and pretend we are twins, Mrs. Ricca is so happy she gives us more clothes. Both Susan and I like our let's pretend game so much that we make look-alike dresses for our look-alike paper dolls. We can't tell them apart.

When I think about it now, I believe that Mrs. Ricca wanted Susan to have a constant playmate. As I was the only other child at Camp the same age as Susan, that playmate was me. But, probably

© KONINKLIJKE BRILL NV, LEIDEN, 2019 | DOI:10.1163/9789004411364_003

even more important was that my father was their lawyer and he had arranged for them to summer at Camp.

Only the mothers and children spend the entire summer at Camp. Fathers stay in Chicago during the week, reuniting with their families on Friday nights. On Saturday nights many parents go to Williams Bay for dining and dancing. On one particular Saturday night in early August, my sixteen-year old sister, Jessica, is baby-sitting Susan. Because Jessica is an experienced sitter and Mother is only eight cottages away, Susan's parents are sanguine about Susan's little headache and tiredness. Jessica could call Mother if necessary and the Riccas could cut their evening short, be home before midnight.

"Help! Dad!" My sister's screams wake-me up. From my top bunk-bed, I can see Jessica running up the gravel pathway.

Father is on the porch, smoking. Mother's asleep.

"It's Susan!" Jessica screams. "She can't move!"

Jessica and Father run down the gravel path to Mallard. I follow. Susan is ash-gray gasping for breath.

"Get Doctor Phillips," Father orders Jessica. "He's in Red Robin."

I watch Susan struggle for breath. I watch my father breathe into her mouth.

When Jessica returns with Dr. Phillips, it is too late. Susan is dead.

"I'll talk to the police," Father says.

"Police?" Jessica shudders.

"Whenever's there's an unexpected death, the police have to come," Father says. "You kids go on back to our cottage."

Jessica and I hold hands on that moonless night as we trudge up the path. Gravel stings my bare toes. I am crying.

"You'll be okay," Jessica says.

I nod. I knew I wasn't going to die, too, because Susan was adopted and I wasn't.

Bulbar polio was the diagnosis. Mallard cabin was closed. Camp was closed. Geneva Lake was closed. Parents had taken their children away from Chicago—away from public pools and water supplies, away from congestion and movie theaters and amusement parks, away from the houses with "Quarantined" placards on them, away from the daily disease count in the *Tribune,* away from the disease that targeted children, putting tens-of-thousands of them at risk for permanent paralysis—or, as in Susan's case, death from the sudden inability to breathe. The rich Riccas had brought their daughter to the presumptive safety of the countryside, the pristine Geneva Lake of Wisconsin. But it didn't work. She was not safe. She was dead.

***

"Do you remember Susan Ricca?" I ask my sister Jessica some fifty-years later.

"That name doesn't ring a bell," Jessica, who never forgets anything, says.

"The little girl that died of bulbar polio at Camp?"

"I don't know anything about that."

"But you were baby-sitting," I say.

"No," she says. "I wasn't there."

"But you were."

"No. I wasn't."

***

As I write this, so many thoughts buzz around in my head. The Riccas were so unlike the other people at camp in attire, demeanor, and displays of wealth and so much like the movie versions of 1940's gangsters that I find myself thinking that Mr. Ricca was a player in Chicago's criminal world. Father was probably his defense attorney. As a criminal attorney, Father devised ways to protect his clients. My father might have found a way for Mrs. Ricca and Susan to be out-of-town because of some bad-business between "families" or to provide an alibi for Mr. Ricca such as *he was at Camp when the crime occurred. See the rental agreement? Ask his wife. Ask his attorney! Ask the restaurant!* Father had told me stories about doing just those kinds of time/place/witness arrangements for his clients. Once he told a client who had phoned him just after he had murdered a "bad cop" to go to the nearby police station immediately and make his presence known; those police testified that the accused could not be guilty because he was "schmoozing" with them at the alleged time of the murder. I don't know the ins-and-outs of the law and I have no idea if what my father did for his clients was legal or not. I do know that Father never lost a defense case. And…well…Chicago.

Oh My God! It has just occurred to me that Mrs. Ricca might have wanted Susan and me to look like twins so that any comeuppance from a rival family could not land on Susan. How would a perp know which child was the Ricca one? The Mafia code prohibited injuring children, especially outside the Families, and surely my father would not have put me in danger. Would he? His defense of an accused murderer entailed him bringing his nine-month pregnant wife, my mother, into the courtroom during the summation. "Gentleman of the jury," he said he said, "I love my wife. And soon I will have my first child. Would I endanger them—emotionally or physically—by bringing them here if my client were guilty of the heinous murders of which he has been accused? Would I?" Of course, he would. And did. But I cannot believe he would consciously put me at risk. But Mrs. Ricca might have been happy to do so.

I Google, "Chicago-crime families—1940's Ricca." I get one-million-two-hundred thousand hits. Wikipedia describes a Paul Ricca as looking like the stereotypical movie mobster and sounding like one, too. According to Wikipedia, his favorite one-liner was, "Make-a him go away."

In 1939 Paul Ricca was underboss of Al Capone's organization, rising to Boss before 1943 and remaining so for the next thirty years. During his tenure, the Capone organization took over the movie projectors union, strong-arming huge pay-offs from the Hollywood movie-business by threatening projectionist strikes. I know my father had Hollywood connections, defended Capone's people, and represented the movie projectionists in court. Susan died the summer Paul Ricca became *Godfather.*

But maybe it was some other Mr. Ricca who had come to camp that summer when Susan died. Maybe, a brother or a cousin, a minor player, Whichever Ricca it was, Father knew, personally, how dangerous the Chicago criminal world was. After Father told "Al"

16

(Capone) to pay his taxes, my parents' house was ransacked and gifts Capone had given father for legal services were missing. But none of the wedding gifts were. Father immediately drove my mother and sister Jessica out of Chicago to Los Angeles where they stayed until Capone was incarcerated for tax-evasion. My father was the only lawyer to survive Capone's wrath.

Given my father's first-hand experiences with the mob, I think it highly likely that he instructed Jessica to deny any connection to the night that Susan Ricca died as a way to protect her from possible recriminations, or worse. My father taught us children to shut-up—to keep secrets. All three of his children—Jessica, Barrie and me—have been really good at that.

Our home phone, a pay phone registered to who knows whom, was also Father's office phone. A plate of nickels was always available should we need to make an outgoing call, and a three-minute egg timer sat next to it—that's as long as we were allowed to "tie-up" the phone. We were never to write down a message, always remember it long enough to tell Father, and, if ever asked, deny knowledge of anything untoward. Of course, Jessica would deny "knowing anything" about little Susan Ricca. And she would have continued to do so throughout her life. She would zip-her-lip. *What else did she "zip her lip" about?*

***

I wonder how Susan's death affected Jessica. What was it like for her to repress the knowledge? To not speak of it? Is that why she devoted her life to helping young children at risk? Is that how she displaced her terror? Is that why she accepted being childless, herself? I cannot know how Jessica processed this horrendous event as the secret-truth has died with her, but I wish I did know.

I know some of how Susan's death affected our family. Jessica never again came to the Lake. We no longer stayed in Bluebird, but moved to a cottage further up the hill. We took the steps, rather than the gravel path past Mallard, down to the lake. The Riccas didn't come to Camp again and they were never mentioned. Father changed law offices.

And I know some of how Susan's death affected me, although I have never talked or written about it before—not because I had repressed the memory, but probably because I had suppressed the trauma. Susan was my age-mate, my only age-mate at camp. We were both smart little girls with fanciful ideas for make-believe and dress-up. We shared showers and popsicles; toys and toilets; bed sheets and bug-dissections.

Mother threw away all the toys, dolls, and clothes Mrs. Ricca had given me. There were no objects to remember Susan by. My little-equal was gone. Sweet Susan didn't infect me with the polio virus. She died. Not me. It could have been me. It *could* have been me, too. Two.

EN GARDE: INGRID

Ingrid Magnusson has the palest and squarest face I have ever seen, and the blondest and straightest hair. Her bangs touch her eyebrows. Mine touch mine. We have the same shoe size. Plus we were both born in the Evangelical Deaconess Hospital on the same summer day at daybreak, within minutes of each other. But we didn't come to know about that until this year.

We are nine years old, best friends and classmates. We can communicate without words. Two quick blinks signal approval, fingering an ear, disapproval.

I often go to Ingrid's house after school. She is an only child. She has no tormenting older brother like I have in my brother, Barrie, and no uncaring sister like I have in my older sister, Jessica. When I was five, they took me to see my first movies, a double-feature— *Frankenstein* and *Frankenstein meets Wolfman.* Barrie told me movie stories were true stories. Jessica told me I couldn't leave my seat. I gasped with terror watching Frankenstein's monster lurching at me.

***

But now, Ingrid and I are going to her apartment after school. Walking down Cornelia is the safest way, but, despite the recent ghastly news, Ingrid likes walking the unsafe way, down Addison, under the elevated tracks, past the *dreaded* catchment grate, past the apartments with the English basements where dark-haired men sit licking tobacco into the shape of cigars and their children call to passers-by, "See-Gar— See-gar-e-yo."

"Mother says they're Gypsies, and they steal children," I tell Ingrid, feeling both fear and excitement as we stand in front of one of the basement windows. Ingrid stares at a man in the window the way a cat stares at a mouse, mesmerizing it, conquering it by force of will. She is

© KONINKLIJKE BRILL NV, LEIDEN, 2019 | DOI:10.1163/9789004411364_004

fearless. "I think he did it," she says. When the man looks away, Ingrid tugs on my arm and we walk on, Ingrid swaggering like a conquering hero, me imitating her, inviting her seeming fearlessness into my body.

"Barrie put me down a catchment grate when I was three years old," I tell Ingrid. "Then he stepped on my fingers." I blink twice, signaling *Yes, I am telling the truth.*

"If you had fallen, you would have broken your neck," Ingrid fingers her ear, signaling *how terrible of him.*

"Father came and saved me. Barrie said he was stepping on my fingers to keep me from falling in."

"What did your mother do?"

"She praised Barrie."

***

Outside Ingrid's apartment door, we take off our shoes and place them in a wooden box. She opens the locked door with the key dangling from a string around her neck. We come in, hang up our coats on a wooden coat rack, traverse the rag-rugs and enter the living room. The walls are white, the curtains yellow and blue. An under-stuffed couch faces the window. Everything is orderly. No devious brother here.

Barrie's spheres of potential treachery have grown a zillion-fold since Father, having decided that Barrie was too shy, arranged for his training to become a magician. When he is nine, he debuts as a boy magician on the television show, Kukla, Fran, and Ollie. He cuts me in half. How it is done is a secret. No one in my family reveals secrets.

Now, Barrie is becoming a mentalist. "Now you see it," he says about the rabbit he drops into the tall black hat. "Now you don't," he says, turning the hat upside down, pulling its brim back.

"You're next, Laurel," he says waving his magician's wand over my head. "Abracadabra! You've disappeared, Laurel."

"No I haven't," I say, patting my left wrist.

"How do you know?" he says, grinning.

How could I know?

"Let's ask Jessica," he says, calling her into the room. "Have you seen Laurel anywhere?"

"No, I sure haven't," Jessica answers. "Has she disappeared again?"

Maybe I have.

"Abracadabra!! " Barrie shouts. "Now you have reappeared... You owe me."

I feel lucky to be in Ingrid's apartment, a life-sized version of the miniature Swedish room displayed at the Art Institute. Lucky lucky me! I am in this actual room with just Ingrid, where nothing disappears and reappears. As Ingrid's mother says, "Everything has a place, and everything is in its place."

Ingrid's and my place is to sit side-by-side on the sofa each silently reading a novel. We almost never talk about what we are reading or about our lives. We are like toddlers engaging in parallel play. How nice it is to have no competitive feelings or scornful words or dangers.

Had my mother seen me she would have approved my quiet and respectful behavior. But, had she seen the Magnusson's décor she would have thought it plain and cheap, although she never would have said so. Mother never said anything bad about anyone as she believed that if one *can't say something nice, one shouldn't say anything at all.*

When Mother was eight-years old, her Russian Jewish mother escaped the pogroms near Kiev and brought her children as passengers in steerage to America to join their father, who had come earlier to earn enough money to send for his family. During the pogroms, Jewish settlements were destroyed, women raped, and men murdered. If my mother did not directly experience these atrocities, she unquestionably knew about them. When I was a grown woman, I asked her to tell me about her life in Russia. "Why would anyone want to know about terrible things," she answered. She would not speak about the "bad" things, but she could not forget them.

No surprise, then, that Mother relished an American upper-middle class life provided by my Gentile father, a successful attorney and (could be) Son of the American Revolution. Mother embraced the symbols of success: brocaded wallpaper, heavily carved and perfectly matched mahogany chairs, credenza and tables, maroon silk damask draperies, an over-stuffed sofa that Father napped on, often with his shoes still on and his Parliament cigarette burning itself out in a cut-crystal ashtray, near the *Tribune* wrinkled on the wall-to-wall carpeting.

"Enough reading," Mrs. Magnusson announces. "Wash up for supper." She sets the blue porcelain table with four white plates and four white paper napkins. Promptly at 5:00 Mr. Magnusson unlocks the back kitchen door, comes in, puts his lunch pail on the counter, nods to his wife and bows to Ingrid and me. He looks like a Viking returning from the forest, and smells like one, too, like freshly cut wood, sawdust, and pine needles. His hands are large, strong looking, gnarled. His pale blue shirt matches his eyes. He talks about the many enemies that the Swedes have overcome—Norwegians, French, Germans. He brags about the Knights Templars, soldiers who were known for their strength and skills in combat. He admonishes Ingrid and me: *You must be able to defend yourself.*

On this evening, we sit down and put our hands in prayer position. "Herre Gud," Mr. Magnusson says and we pray silently for what seems like an eternity until he says, "Amen." I pray to be fearless like Ingrid and strong like Mr. Magnusson. Mrs. Magnusson passes plates of kracklebread, buttered cucumbers, boiled potatoes, and little fishes.

"You must eat six kracklebread a day to be strong," she says to me. She smiles. I feel special and cared about. "That's how many Ingrid eats. All the children need to be strong, now."

"Drink your tea," Mrs. Magnusson says at the end of our meal. "Rose-hip gives you strong bones. You need strong bones, now."

Mr. Magnusson makes a stabbing gesture into the air, as if he is holding a sword. He shakes his head and says, "And they still haven't found that maniacal dismemberer."

Like every other girl on the north side of Chicago, I am extremely frightened. The *Tribune* has devoted so many pages and pictures to the story. A little girl—Suzanne Degnan—only six years old, but my weight—kidnapped from her bedroom, strangled, and then—Oh, no!—dismembered. That is the word spoken over and over again by the radio announcer. By the adults congregating on the sidewalk. By my school teacher.

Suzanne's blond head had been found in a sewer, at first looking to the police officers like a doll's head. One of her legs, still in its blue pajama bottom, was found in the catchment basin under the El tracks near my home. The other leg in a nearby sewer. Her arms had not yet been found. Suzanne had lived a mile from my home, in Edgewater Beach, my favorite destination. The "maniacal dismemberer" is still out there. That is how he is described in the paper, on the radio, in the school assembly. And now by Mr. Magnusson.

***

Mr. Magnusson twists his wrist in the air, stabs forward, as if trying to skewer someone or something. He gets up and motions for Ingrid and me to follow him into the grown-ups bedroom. He unlocks a painted chest, takes out a wooden box and opens it. "These are the medals I have won during my fencing career," he tells me. Ingrid nods. She knows about these gleaming crosses on multicolored ribbons. He reaches into the bottom of the chest, past a passel of white clothes and removes two swords.

"Those are his foil and epee," Ingrid says.

"These are tools with which to defend yourself," Mr. Magnusson says."Take the foil in your hand, Laurel."

I hesitate.

"You are right-handed aren't you? Like Ingrid?"

I fidget as I decide how best to answer his question. Father had turned me into a right hander by not allowing me to eat, write or draw with my left hand so I wasn't sure if I was still really a left-hander or not. But I wanted to be so I take the plunge and blurt-out, "Left handed!"

"Are you sure you are left handed?"

"I am sure—I sure want to be." I am telling the truth. I double-blink my eyes.

"Very good! You and Ingrid are mirror-images of each other. You match up very well. You look to be the same heights, weights, girths."

"And shoe size," Ingrid and I say in unison.

"*En garde!*" he says. He lunges two steps forward and one back. He is enticing us through body movements. He twists his wrist and lunges forward again. He looks fearless. Ingrid and I double blink. We are in agreement.

"Can you train us to be fencers?" I ask, amazed at my boldness. I rarely ask anyone for anything. "Will you?"

"If your parents agree, Laurel. I will train you at the Swedish fencing club. You and Ingrid will be my fencing-twins."

***

My family is sitting in our places at the dining room table. I rub my red and swollen thumb. Earlier Barrie had pulled it to make me release my grip on my bag of purees, the most sought after marbles because they made the best shooters in marble games. He sold them back to me before dinner. Mother has noticed my red thumb and asks, accusingly, "What have you been doing?" Barrie glares at me. I recognize the wide-eyed look that proceeds his counting slowly to ten. On the count of ten I will be hypnotized. "My thumb got caught in my marble bag," I say telling the partial truth.

I push a bit of roast beef around with my DuraGold fork on my gold-rimmed plate, wedding gifts from Al Capone to my parents. Gravy drips through the lace table-cloth onto the dining room table. I sit on my left hand.

Poncho, our rescued toothless Chihuahua, is begging for food. Barrie gives him a little kick. Poncho snarls. Jessica exchanges milk glasses with me—hers full, mine empty. Our parents don't notice. Or care.

The time seems right to ask my father whether I can take fencing lessons with my friend, Ingrid Magnusson, at the Swedish Club. Father puts his lit cigarette in the cut-glass ashtray near his plate and takes a swallow of scotch. "That club would be in Swedetown," he says. "That's a good area…safe…The Swedes don't look for trouble— except with the Norwegians."

Barrie laughs.

"Probably Magnusson is in the Knights Templar," Father continues. He lights another Parliament from the lit one. He scans our faces, preparing to lecture us. Father, knows *everything* or everything he has ever read because he has a photographic memory. He says that's how he got through law school so fast. He never had to learn case law; he only had to remember where cases were located in the law volumes. Besides which, he never intended to do anything other than jury trials and that mostly required charming the jury. He always did.

"During the Dark Ages," Father clears his throat. "The Knights Templar were a military order providing warriors for the Crusades... The French King Phillip accused them of heresy and tax evasion...He had them arrested...And burnt them at the stake."

"We're eating, Tyrrell," Mother says.

"Tell some more, Father," Barrie says, taunting Poncho with a rib-bone.

"The Templars have had a lot of enemies over the centuries but the Swedes always fight back. In Chicago, we know them as a hard-working people—mostly in the trades...carpenters and painters... most of them devoted Christians...actually, they are kind of modern day Christian Soldiers...*marching as to war, with the...*"

Our rat-terrier Happy howls along with Father's singing. Jessica gives Happy a piece of my Wonder Bread crust. Poncho grabs it. Barrie shoves Poncho. Mother forks a green-bean.

"So is Ingrid's Father some kind of big-shot soldier?" Barrie asks, flexing his muscles and eyeing me. He has used those muscles on me before. Twice he blind-folded me and tied me down so his Boy Scout troop could prepare for their first-aid badges. Mother thought Barrie was learning to be helpful. To this day, the thought of being strapped down makes my gut cramp. I would not let my obstetrician strap me to the table during the birth of my first son. I cannot watch television programs that dramatize women being blindfolded and restrained. And, I cannot stand my feet being pinned down by a top sheet or blanket. I kick.

"I've seen lots of Mr. Magnusson's medals and swords, Barrie," I say.

"Why are you so eager to learn to fence, Laurel?" Mother asks.

"I *need* to."

Barrie eyes me.

"To defend myself."

"From what?" Mother asks.

Barrie starts counting under his breath. I look away.

"That bad man is still out there," I say. "You never know."

Barrie stops counting.

"Fencing is a good sport for a lady," Father says, apparently missing my point. "Yes. You can add fencing lessons to your equestrian ones." He taps his pinkie ring on the table.

"Mr. Magnusson will take you there and back?" Mother asks.

"Yes." I straighten my shoulders, and sit tall.

Mother shrugs her shoulders and puts her linen napkin on the table. A signal for us children to recite our words of gratitude, "Mother, excuse me and thank you for the lovely meal." Father's nod releases us and we children put our linen napkins on our plates, push back our chairs and rise. I go to my bedroom, close the door, and look in vain for my bag of purees.

***

On the following Saturday morning, Mr. Magnusson, Ingrid, and I take the bus West to Clark Street, a neighborhood that is new and foreign to me. The Swedish Gymnasium and Fencing Club, restaurants, cafes, taverns fly the yellow and blue flags of Sweden. Sweet smells mix with fishy ones. What look like families of Vikings are eating cakes and talking in a lilting language that seems to end each sentence as if it were a question.

We enter the Club. "First, you must be strengthened," Mr. Magnusson tells us and he begins our training:

"Squat, hold, rise...squat, hold, rise...deeper...squat..."

"Ankle twist...push-up...crunch...shoulder stretch...row..."

"Lunge...right leg forward...left leg forward...balance... balance...balance..."

"Squat quickly...stretch...push from toes...explode!"

'Lunge from toes...explode...retreat!"

"Focus. Remember fencing is both a mind and a body sport."

"Violence without proper technique is shameful," Mr. Magnusson tells us after we've been sufficiently strengthened to start our fencing lessons. He is dressed completely in black, the tradition for judges and referees. Ingrid and I look like little knights or oddly dressed angels after we don our white fencing uniforms—gloves, jacket, knickers, socks and shoes. But our masks prevent us from seeing each other's eyes.

"This will be your foil," Mr. Magnusson says handing the foil to my left hand. "The blade is sharp and there is a button that covers the point. That protects you and your opponent…Here, try it."

I feel the thrill of holding the foil in my left hand, the wrist guard protecting my wrist, my wrist steady and strong, my wrist agile, my wrist connecting to my fingers and to my arm and my shoulder to my whole body. I feel whole and empowered—powerful enough to go against my father's wishes, to claim to be myself: a left-hander. I feel invincible. I am a Girl Warrior.

Ingrid and I face-off—*en garde*—on the fencing strip. We practice our wrist twists, lunges, retreats but now with foils in our hands. We learn the language—lunge, parry, riposte, engage, touch, prêt, arret—in our heads and our bodies. *Attack…Defend…Attack* until your foil touches the torso of your opponent—*touch*—and then do it again. Do it five times. At the conclusion of our practicing, Mr. Magnusson reminds us that fencing is a mind and body sport.

The first registered duel between Ingrid and me goes on interminably—neither of us can score the five touches with the requisite two touch difference. Our bodies and skills are evenly matched and we have been trained by the same Master. I finally figure out the only way to win is to out-wit her. I do that by requesting a break, taking off my mask, and blinking twice at her, our secret way of saying "*yes*," followed by fingering my ear, our way of saying "*no*." Maybe she felt that I knew something she didn't—or maybe my contradictory messages distract her—but she loses her concentration. Two lateral parries and the duel is mine.

There is something Kafkaesque about this. My friend, Ingrid, who once sat peacefully beside me, each of us silently reading, has become my combatant. On the fencing strip we are opponents, competitors. I want to touch her torso with the point of my foil. Five times. I want to win. I want her to lose. I want her father to recognize my superiority, her inferiority. I need to show that I am the superior twin.

But perhaps, though, the side-by-side silent reading and the foil-to-torso activities are more similar than I realized. I was probably more competitive in our side-by-side reading than I acknowledged at the time. *Am I turning pages faster than Ingrid? Have I read more books than Ingrid?* I imagine I kept count. By not talking or sharing our feelings or opinions about anything, we created a faux intimacy. I didn't come to know her in the girly ways I had known other friends—sharing secrets, chocolates, and ChapStick. Given the distant, controlled, and silent way we related on the sofa we could have been two boys.

I think that's what we were like—"boy friends." It was easy, then, to transform my latent competitiveness into an overt one on the fencing strip. It was safe on the strip to harness my suppressed rage and let it rip. On the strip, I was enacting how I might protect the actual little girl in danger that I was. On the sofa and on the strip, I had discovered the boy way of doing friendship, tamping down gentler feelings while heightening those that proved one was stronger, heartier, and more likely to survive. I was enacting what I had heard the combat soldiers say about the war: *kill or be killed.*

"I am proud of you, Laurel," Mr. Magnusson says. "The foil is yours to keep."

"May I take it home?" I ask. I am beside myself with joy.

"It is *yours.*"

"Mine!"

***

Tap...tap...tap...

"Who's there?" I am in bed, in my bedroom near the kitchen back door. My door is closed.

"Lau...rel." A raspy voice calls my name.

"Go away!"

"Lau...rel, I'm coming for you."

"Go away! Barrie, Stop it!"

I have gone to bed extremely frightened. Suzanne Degnan's maniacal dismemberer is still out there. Suzanne's sister is my age.

The newspaper quoted her as saying, "It should have been me…I should have taken care of my little sister…It is my fault…If I had stayed in the room with her, it would not have happened to her…I left her alone." Her parents let her say all those things to the reporter. *If I had a sister, would I feel that way? I do feel that way…I don't know why…*

"That sneaky Suzanne…that fat girl…she was only my warm-up…I wanted her sister…and now I'm coming for you." Barrie pushes open my door. He has a nylon stocking over his face and he has pulled his shoulders up so that he looks and moves like Frankenstein's monster. He waves something that looks like a stick at me. He rasps, "This is Suzanne's left arm."

"Get out of here!" I yell. "Stop! You're scaring me."

***

"You hit your brother on his back with your sword?" Mother asks me.

"My foil. Yes."

"He was bleeding."

"Yes."

"You hit him more than once?"

"Yes. Five Times."

"Say you're sorry."

"No."

"Apologize."

"No."

Mother takes away my foil, cancels my fencing tournaments, and grounds me. No more Ingrid, my fencing twin. No more safe haven at the Magnusson's. No more left handed sport.

***

Frightening months pass before Suzanne Degnan's murderer is arrested. During that time, parents and teachers monitor children and restrict our freedom of movement. The boogie-man is somewhere out there, living amongst us. *Don't talk to strangers*, my mother says whenever I leave the house, as if not talking to strangers could protect me. Has she forgotten that Suzanne was kidnapped from her house? That her house was not safe? *Walk away from the curbs*, Mother says, as if that would protect me from the maniac who is hiding in the bushes, the doorways, the alleys…my house.

***

The horror of Suzanne Degnan's death, the aftermath of contagious fear, my loss of a twinnish-friend/foil/left hand strength, and the terror my brother inflicted on me have stayed with me all these years, as have the scars I can still see on my brother's back.

Barrie and I are in our fifties, sitting in our bathing suits on his pier at Torch Lake. My husband, Ernest, and I are celebrating July Fourth with Barrie and his wife, Nancy.

"He was so annoying," Barrie says, taking up a storyline he began earlier. "That raccoon would look at me with his beady eyes, tempting me. I'd yell at him but he just came back. So, I rigged a net off the pier and caught him."

"So where'd you take him?" I ask. I'd had a troublesome raccoon some years ago. We used a Have-a-Heart trap and released him in Highbanks Metro Park.

"I took him," Barrie says, "to the public boat launch. I tied rocks to the net and tossed that sucker in the lake."

"You mean you drowned him. Live?"

Barrie laughs. Nancy nods and says, "We shouldn't annoy Barrie."

"And those squirrels are really annoying me, now," he continues. "I'm going to get my B-B gun to take care of them."

"You're kidding?" I ask.

"He's serious," Ernest says.

I think of the hammers and rocks and toys Barrie threw at me when we were children. I gag remembering the stick he stuck down my throat.

Barrie gets up and I see his scarred back.

"I gave you those back scars," I say. I cock my head as If I am looking for a fight.

"I know," he says. "I deserved them."

"Why were you so awful?" I ask, gratified that he has owned his boyhood behavior. "And why are you still so awful?"

"Lots of reasons," he says.

"Tell me!"

"Nah. Let's not talk about bad stuff? C'mon, I'll race you to the life raft."

***

I read a clipping from the *Tribune* and learn that a cross of forget-me-nots lay atop Suzanne Degnan's small white coffin, and that the flowers "danced in the wind" as the coffin was lowered into a tiny grave at All Saints Catholic Cemetery.

I dream a beautiful grown-up woman stands before me whose arms have been severed above her elbows. I want to help her—I want to reattach that which had been dismembered.

MIRROR/MIRROR: LAUREL/LAUREL

Seventeen year old William Heirens is arrested for Suzanne Degnan's. murder. The Chicago police interrogate him the way Chicago police do depriving the accused of sleep, water, food, phone calls. Under the influence of truth-serum, Heirens talks of an alternate personality named *George*. "An imaginary friend," say the psychiatrists. "Preparing for an insanity defense," says the prosecutor's office. "A Dr. Jekyll and Mr. Hyde," says the *Tribune*. Front page photos of Heirens, one with hair combed and one with hair mussed are proof. Heirens is found guilty by the *Tribune*. Suzanne Degnan is buried without her arms. Case *closed.* I am safe again outside, alone, in this late summer of 1946.

I have often window-shopped at the Edgewater's *Tween Shop* but now I am going inside with my tenth-year birthday money on my first solo shopping trip. My post-war Schwinn (a rarity probably obtained on the black market by my father) leans on the brick storefront. The bike's wire basket glints in the sun. The combination lock's left dangling and open like the locks now again left open on our front door, back door and Father's Studebaker.

Father is rarely home for dinner but on week-ends he takes me to the Chicago Theater. I feel special and grown-up taking in plays and musicals, dressed up and up way past my bedtime. Often a particular woman sits beside my father or behind him. Sometimes, she and I chat. Many years later she comes to my father's funeral. She tells me those theater outings were an opportunity for her to "see me," father's "favorite," and to "be part of his *other* life." She shows me a photograph of her son, *Richard,* a spitting image of my father. "You and Richard would like each other," she says.

Jessica is off to college in Iowa. I am glad she is gone and that her bossy boyfriend is gone, too, off to a war. Staring into her empty bedroom with its wagon-wheel themed maple furniture and frothy

© KONINKLIJKE BRILL NV, LEIDEN, 2019 | DOI:10.1163/9789004411364_005

coverlets and curtains, I wonder how a sister of mine could have such corny taste. Barrie, has added new interests—basketball, girls, and sailboats. His magician skills have expanded. I think he mesmerizes his women teachers. His grades improve.

"May I help you?" the tall woman standing beside the cash register at the *Tween Shop* asks. Her hair is in a bun and her fingernails are long and scarlet. If I worked in such a store, I could have a bun and scarlet nails, too. Between us is a glass-covered banquet of under-things for tween-aged girls, like myself—or how I like to think of myself, now that I am ten and will have classes on the third-floor of Le Moyne School, like the eleven, twelve and thirteen years olds.

"Lots of the girls like this set," the woman says, tapping her nails and pointing to a lacy baby-pink training-bra and panty-girdle. She sees from my frown that I am not like *lots of girls*. "Perhaps, you would like this white-set?" she says, pointing to some cotton-knits. My frown deepens.

"That," I say. "Those." I am lusting after the turquoise and pink plaid bra and garter belt. I blush from embarrassment and excitement.

"We just got those in…They are on spec," the tall woman says.

"I don't see any specks," I say.

"No…no…no. Not dots. These are designer lingerie."

She looks me up and down. "Why not try them on?"

***

Alone in a private dressing room with a three-way-mirror, I can see myself straight-on and I can see my sides and I can see my behind. There are no full-length mirrors anywhere in my house. I have never seen my backside before. I have only seen my front-side in the fun-house that makes everyone look round or stringy. The largest mirror is on the bathroom medicine cabinet where I look at my face while I brush my teeth. I have never seen how I look naked.

Early lessons created in my mind the idea of God as a dirty old man, who sees me all the time, even when I am not dressed. A God who *wants* to see me! So, I have taught myself how to dress and undress—under sheets or in the closet–so God would never see me naked. I would never be naked. Even the word—*naked*—felt, well, naked. I look at naked me.

"Who are you?" I whisper to the Girl-in-the Mirrors. I am mesmerized. She seems so real and so *almost* me, but not quite. Her body is straight as a plank; her arms thin branches; her skinny legs don't touch in three places—thigh, upper calf, lower calf. Her knees are knobby and so are her ankles and elbows. Her angel bones protrude. So do her hip bones and collar bones. She has a large breast-bud swelling up her right nipple. I touch my right nipple and feel for the breast-bud that is not there. She does the same touching her left nipple.

Could there be a "good me" and a "bad me"?

"I bet you are right handed," I whisper to Her, waving my left hand. We smile. "Listen," I murmur, "if you were here, I don't think Father would have done this to me."

"Done what?"

"Not let me use my left hand."

"Mean," She says.

"You have no idea what it is like to be sitting on the hand you want to use."

"Awful."

"I broke my left arm ice-skating when I was six. I thought God was punishing me for trying to use it. Father wrapped it in a torn sheet and didn't let me go to the doctor to have it set."

"Terrible!"

"My arm healed crooked."

"Oh no!"

"Mother took me to a doctor, secretly. He put an awful smell up my nose so I'd be asleep when he rebroke it. He put me in a white plaster cast from my thumb to my elbow."

I see tears.

"Father was angry at me and Mother."

"Well, I am furious at him for making you suffer."

"Every day is a challenge," I say. "I don't know how things work—keys, handles, doors. I get lost all the time."

"Why did he do this to you?"

"Father says, 'It's a right-handed world.' He wants me to fit in."

"Everything all right in there?" The tall woman's crimson nails tat-a-tat on the door.

"Fine."

"Does the lingerie fit?"

"Perfect."

CHAPTER 6

LIAR-LIAR: LEAH

Nearly every Saturday night at six o'clock our first-floor tenants, Mr. and Mrs. Bernstein, go out for dinner and dancing. And nearly every Saturday night, I baby-sit with Leah, their five-year-old chubby-chubby daughter. I am eleven.

Three-weeks have passed since I last baby-sat Leah. Now, it is 5:55 and I hop down the three flights of stairs from our top-floor apartment to the Bernstein's. Mrs. Bernstein greets me and disappears into her bedroom. She has set the table for Leah and me with cheese sandwiches, milk, and lots of cookies. Leah eats most of the cookies and I clear the table, wash the dishes, and put them on a rack to dry. I am never to put them away in the cabinet as I might put these kosher dairy dishes mistakenly in with the kosher meat dishes.

My job includes feeding Leah supper, playing with her, getting her ready for bed, sleeping in Leah's other bed, setting our alarm clock, getting Leah up and dressed in the morning, feeding us toast and juice, taking Leah with me to Anshe Emet Sunday School and bringing her back home afterwards, by which time her mother would be awake, in the kitchen in her bathrobe and curlers. For this I earn $1.25.

"How do we look?" Mrs. Bernstein asks me before leaving for the evening out. She is chubbier than anyone in my family and wears lots of make-up. Her high-heel shoe color matches her fancy dress, as does Mr. Bernstein's tie. He is chubby, too.

"Like you two belong together," I say.

"Now you be good, Leah, and listen to what Laurel tells you," Mrs. Bernstein says. "Laurel, you can call your mother if you need any help."

This Saturday night begins as it always does with Leah and me playing *Sorry,* Crazy-Eights, and doll-house dolls. But Leah is wound-up. She scrambles the *Sorry* cards with the Crazy-Eight ones.

© KONINKLIJKE BRILL NV, LEIDEN, 2019 | DOI:10.1163/9789004411364_006

She throws the doll-house furniture into the waste-basket. She jumps on her bed. Jump! Jump! Jump!

"Stop jumping and get into your pajamas!" I command. "Or, I will call my mother and you'll be sorry!"

"Help me?" she whines, trying to pull her still buttoned blouse over her head. "Ha! Ha! You can't see me," she says, whirling around like a cat in a paper bag.

"Hold still," I say and help her out of her clothes and into her pajamas. Her body feels squishy. *So that's how fat feels.*

She begins her crazy jumping again. Jump! Jump! Jump!

"Stop it," I yell.

"I'm a twin!" Leah yells back. "I'm a twin!"

"No, you're not."

"Twin! Twin! Twin!"

"Stop it! Stop lying!"

"Twin! I'm a twin…twin…twin…"

***

When Leah and I get back the next morning from Sunday School, Mrs. Bernstein is sitting at the kitchen table in her housecoat and plushy house shoes. Leah runs into her bedroom. I have not spoken to her all morning.

"I am not going to sit for you anymore," I tell Mrs. Bernstein.

"But why, Laurel? Do you want us to pay you more?"

"No." I hesitate. "It is because Leah tells lies."

"What lies, Laurel?"

"She told me she is a twin."

Mrs. Bernstein gets up from her chair, goes into the living room and comes back with a photo-album. She opens it. I glance down at the baby pictures of Leah and then some toddler pictures. Leah is much thinner in those pictures. Mrs. Bernstein turns the pages of the photo-album. Now Leah has a blank look on her face, her eyes seem off kilter, and her top lip looks split. She is still thin. Almost wiry. She looks about four but can scarcely hold her head up.

There is a photo of two Leahs—a chubby one and a skinny one. Under that photo Mrs. Bernstein has written, "Happy Fifth Birthday— Leah and Rachel!"

I am struggling to take it in. *Is there another version of me somewhere?*

"Rachel has been in a special home for children," Mrs. Bernstein tells me. "Last week we told Leah about her twin and they met each other. We thought it was the right time. Leah has been asking us to have another baby."

"Why isn't Rachel living here?" I don't understand. I had heard of children in orphanages when they had no parents, but Rachel has parents and a twin sister.

"Rachel was born with difficulties...Her brain did not develop...She, ah, has trouble with her body...She, ah, can't sit up or walk...or talk...and we visit her every Saturday night when we go out...It is better for her to be in the special home..."

"How better?" My mind imagines the horrors of a mad-house for sick children run by a wicked matron.

"She has nursing care...Anshe Emet sends volunteers...Your mother is one."

"My mother?"

Mrs. Bernstein nods.

"If there are all these helpers, why not have them help here at your home?" I ask.

Do I have a damaged twin living in that special home? Is my Mother is really visiting *her*?

"It would be good if she could be home," Mrs. Bernstein says. "But we can't do it. There are laws that forbid people from being in public whose looks or movements might offend or frighten people. They're called 'Ugly Laws.' Can you imagine how Leah would feel? People turning away from her sister, saying awful things?"

"My father is a lawyer," I say. "He can get that law changed."

"You're very sweet, Laurel," Mrs. Bernstein says. "But the truth is we brought Leah to meet Rachel because Rachel's heart is giving out. She doesn't have long to live."

**

"Mrs. Bernstein told you all of that?" My mother asks.

"Yes."

"She should be ashamed."

Father sells the apartment building. We move.

BLOOD SISTERS: VALERIE

A new girl, Valerie moves into our school district and into my seventh-grade classroom.

We are both tall and skinny with dark-brown bangs and pony-tails. We both love cats and dogs and painting and reading, especially books about horses and girl detectives. Her penmanship is flawless while mine is labored. We reason it is because she is a natural born right-hander while I have been turned into one.

We dress alike, deciding before we say good-bye what we will wear the next day—usually jeans with one leg rolled up higher than the other, a Ship-and-Shore white blouse and our "JUGS" (Just Us Girls) sailor hat, with the rim half-turned up. We both wear glasses, but only when we want to see something. We are both teacher's pets. We often grade our classmates' papers and enter the scores into the grade book. There we discover Valerie and I have the same I.Q.

We are best friends.

Valerie lives in a carriage house up the street from me. In her entry way there is a painting of an exotic cat named Catalina. Her eyes follow me as I go up the stairs, which I do nearly every afternoon after school, and her eyes follow me out the door when I leave. Under Catalina's magical gaze, I feel welcomed and protected.

Valerie's father pops popcorn and makes lemonade for us. He treats us like twins—setting us up on side-by-side work-tables for chemistry and geology projects, sending us on hunts for flora specimens in the backyard. He talks to us about scientific discoveries in his deep radio-announcer voice, for that is his night job and why he is home in the afternoons. He is the kind of hands-on engaged father that for me only exists in Nancy Drew mysteries.

Valerie and I prick our left hand thumbs with a rose-bush thorn. When a little blood trickles, we hold our thumbs against each other's,

© KONINKLIJKE BRILL NV, LEIDEN, 2019 | DOI:10.1163/9789004411364_007

sharing blood, stopping the bleeding. "Valerie," I say, "I give myself a middle-name. Your name. From now on I am *Laurel Valerie*."

***

I am forty years old. I am at my Artist's Way group where we are showing the one object we would save if our house were on fire. I have brought a music-box movement. The metal is slightly rusted, the wood slightly slivered, and the mechanism slightly catawampus. "This was given to me by my best friend Valerie before she moved to the country when we were twelve," I say. "I never saw her again after that but the mechanism still plays." I turn the key and out comes a tinkly *Lullaby and Goodnight*. "I don't play it very often, because I have this superstition that when it no longer plays, I will die."

***

Not quite a year later, I receive a letter from Albuquerque. I can quote it by heart: *"Are you the Laurel Richardson who lived on Cornelia Avenue? If so, I hope you remember me and recognize my name. If not, I apologize for troubling you."* I recognize the name, the politeness, and the flawless penmanship. It is signed *Valerie*.

Valerie has seen me on the *Today Show*, where I was promoting my book, *The New Other Woman: Single Woman Involved with Married Men*.

"I'll be Santa Fe in March," I scrawl back. "I fly into Albuquerque!"

Valerie meets my plane. We both have cat-eye glasses on our heart-shaped faces. She still wears her hair in bangs and a pony-tail. I have a pixie-cut. She is a wrinkled version of her twelve-year-old self. I doubt she has grown an inch. I have grown ten. I bend down to hug her. My Liz Claiborne blouse brushes against her L.L. Bean shirt.

"It's not far to my *casa*," Valerie says as I settle into the passenger seat of her red pick-up truck. She drives to a barrio and points to a small adobe house on a small plot of gravel next to other small adobe houses. Huge trash bins end the row. A broken stove sits next to the bins. "I'm still safe here," she says. "I don't know for how long…the next street over is not safe…but, I try to stay friendly and give the kids gum."

I drive a Dodge Dart and live in a suburb where frame houses rest on quarter acre lots with grass growing all around. Personal trash cans and recycle bins are hidden and backyards fenced. Children play and friendly dogs yap. I moved here from the city a dozen years ago after the teen-aged neighbor boy, on PCP, sledge-hammered his sister's car, demolished my front door, and tried to rape me. The police said I had a choice: shoot him or move. I moved.

"Come on in." Valerie unbolts her double-bolted door. On the entry wall, staring right at me is the painting of Catalina, the exotic cat with the magical eyes.

"O.M.G.!" I say. I watch Catalina's eyes follow me into Valerie's living room.

"You remember the picture?" Valerie says. "Dad thought I might need Catalina's eyes on me!"

Seeing Catalina seeing me I feel at home. At home with Valerie. We could be twelve years old again, but we aren't. We are grown women whose "destinies" have been similar, but different. I am a married sociologist studying the lives of single women who choose long-term relationships with married men. Valerie is a never-married anthropologist who is living that life.

"My dissertation was unfinished," she tells me, "but I couldn't resist the opportunity to go with my advisor to an archeological site in New Mexico."

I know what is coming next. I have interviewed dozens of single women involved with married men.

"We were pretty isolated…and I thought the affair would be a temporary thing…that it fit in with my professional plans."

I feel bad for Valerie in a way I never had for other women that I interviewed. Listening to her hurts me. She had been my best-friend.

"I haven't talked about it to anyone…certainly not my father…"

I nod. My compassion for her expands for I know she is about to tell me the worst part of her story.

"I didn't finish my dissertation, and the affair lasted two decades. He didn't want to leave his wife and I couldn't break it off.

He needed me…I needed him…I didn't have friends or contacts…I needed the job, too…And I loved the work."

"And now?" I ask.

"He died," she says. She looks more bitter than sad. "The archeological site is closed…I have no PhD…I have no job…The funeral was for family only."

She doesn't cry; I don't try to comfort her. We sit side-by-side, quietly, as we did when we were children solving complex math problems, each in our own way.

"What's this?" I ask. I pick up a fairly long brownish-gray artifact.

"It's a Phallic Pestle," Valerie says. "It's quite rare."

"I am so tactile." I rub my hand over the pestle.

"So am I," Valerie says. "That was a major perk of my job. I got to touch everything."

"It is so smooth," I say.

"It's smooth from many years of use in ancient times," she says. "But, here, feel the diamond shaped incision pattern under the double ring."

I pick up a small, rippled concave artifact. "What's this?" I ask.

"That's also very rare," Valerie says. "It polished pins and needles that were made of broken bones."

We spend the afternoon touching artifacts. Catalina watches us.

"Good to see you, Valerie."

"You, too."

I rub my index finger over my left wrist and say, "I still have the music-box movement you gave me."

"I don't remember that."

***

We send Christmas cards back and forth. She sends a generic Christmas letter signed, "Val."

The music box sits on my bedroom table. I play it now and then.

MISS ESTHER

Esther Levine, a square faced and curly haired girl joins my eighth grade class at LeMoyne Grade School. She is a transfer from Girls Latin, the private school that I so wanted to attend. Father nixed it because he believes in public education, and Girls Latin nixed it by refusing to consider me for the scholarship I had secretly applied for. "Your father is an attorney," the cranky woman told me when I phoned about it. "He can afford the tuition."

Esther is the last chosen in gym for relay races—maybe because she is new or because she moves so disjointedly or because I haven't chosen her or maybe for all those reasons since we are the age where, according to *Seventeen*, we can be mean girls. But after gym class, I gush all over Esther.

"I'd love to be going to Girls Latin," I say.

"Be happy that you're not," Esther says. "You'd have to wear a plaid jumper and jacket, and look like everyone else."

"What colors?" I ask, imagining myself in burgundy and white, plaid.

"You'd have to learn Latin."

"I'd love that."

"Are you smart?" Esther cocks her head and stares at me as if she'll be able to see whether I am.

"Yes." I pat the top of my head.

"Will you help me if I need help?" Esther smiles and pats my head.

"Be glad to as long as you don't *copy* my work."

***

Esther lives in the twenty-story high-rise on the corner of Cornelia and Lake Shore Drive. When I was seven years old, my brother, Barrie,

© KONINKLIJKE BRILL NV, LEIDEN, 2019 | DOI:10.1163/9789004411364_008

had convinced me to walk on the building's roof, on top of its narrow gutter boards, while he stood on the corner charging his friends to watch me. One windy day, I looked down. I still have a fear of heights. But, I feel safe here inside Esther's nineteenth floor apartment with its lavish closed draperies, lush carpet, and so many rooms that there is no room for another apartment on her floor.

"Where's your mother?" I ask.

"Vacation."

"Where's your father?"

"A different vacation."

"So who takes care of you?"

"Mahalia. She has her own room and bathroom off the kitchen."

A small dark-skinned woman, Mahalia, sets bright white plates and shiny silverware on snack tables. She gives us sliced apples in caramel dip and pours our milk. She calls me Miss Laurel.

"Here's all the information you need to know about Brazil," I say to Esther handing her a library book. Miss Chambers has assigned Esther to research that South American country. I have Argentina.

"Have you read the Brazil book?" Esther asks.

"I've put book-marks on the few pages you'll need," I say.

"Will I have to *read* them?" Esther whines. "Can't you just tell me what they say?"

I wonder if this friendship can go anywhere. We certainly can't bond over books.

"Do you want to see my mother's room?" Esther asks.

Esther's mother has her own bedroom. One wall is covered with mirrored doors. Two dressers hold ornate jewelry boxes, a vanity with a plushy cushion chair holds a third box.

"C'mon," Esther says. "Take your pick." She flings open the mirrored doors. Behind them are Mrs. Levine's clothes—fur coats, floor length formals, party dresses, tweeds. Shoes. Scarves. Boas. Hats.

"What do you mean?"

"C'mon!" Esther takes a burgundy silk gown off its hanger and holds it up to my chin. "An okay color for you." She takes a royal blue gown off its hanger. "This is my favorite," she says. She undresses to her under things. She gestures for me to undress, too. I do. She slips the blue gown over her head and I slip the burgundy one over mine. I like fancy clothes, especially gowns. Maybe Esther and I can become fashion friends. If not now, maybe when we're grown-ups.

"Let's see," she says, appraising me. "This would look good." She wraps a feather boa around my neck. Around her neck she wraps a white-fox. It has four fox feet and a fox head biting its fox tail. She grabs two pairs of silver high-heel barely-there strappy-sandals. "Try these on," she says, handing me a pair and putting the other pair on her own feet. My toes stick out the sides and front. Esther's don't. "We'll teeter-totter like toddler-twins," Esther says.

"We don't need hats," she says. "But we do need jewelry." I join her in rifling through Mrs. Levine's jewelry boxes. "Don't worry," Esther says. "The really good stuff is in the safe."

We prance in front of the mirrors, take gemstone rings off and on, and I answer Esther's questions about Brazil.

Mahalia looks in on us. "Anything you need, Miss Esther?"

"I want to show Laurel the ballroom," Esther says.

"What ballroom?" I ask.

Esther points above her head.

Mahalia touches the skeleton key she has on a string around her neck.

"Mahalia has to bring us," Esther says. "I can't imagine why."

We walk back through the sprawling apartment. On the walls are framed commendations for Mr. Levine's contribution to the war effort. He made soldiers' uniforms. I hope they weren't the shoddy ones my tailor grandfather called *shmates.*

We leave through a back-door and climb the stairs until we reach a pair of gilded doors. Mahalia opens one door with the skeleton key. "Miss Esther, I wait here for you and Miss Laurel."

Esther and I dance our way into a palatial space. I imagine the balls, dances, and parties that have been held in this room. I imagine beautiful people in beautiful clothes dancing to beautiful music.

My eyes are restless. So many details. Rectangles, zigzags and, then, deer jumping over each other in a fairy tale garden, nymphs hiding from Pan, and floor to ceiling windows, looking onto the unending ocean of Lake Michigan. When I close my eyes, I pretend I am with a handsome boy, who will someday get down on his knee and ask me to marry him, and, to encourage his ardor I will have dabbed *Evening in Paris* behind my ears, on my wrists and between my breasts. My pulse points. I twirl, twirl, twirl. Oh, how I would love to come to a party here!

***

I invite Esther to join my Just Us Girls Club. If she joins, there will be four Jewish girls and four Gentile ones with me—half Jewish and half Gentile—being the fulcrum. In my most deliriously ambitious moments, I imagine that I am the model-maker for harmony between the Jewish and Gentile peoples of the world.

Esther helps organize the Club's rummage sale in my basement. She brings bags of knick-knacks and some silk-scarves she says her mother is tired of. I part with my favorite white-glass sitting hen. We raise $81.00 for poor children. Our pictures and names are on the front page of the *Sun Times.* The famous columnist, Irv Kupcinet, features us in Kup's Column, probably because my father, one of Kup's Scotch-drinking buddies at the men's only Berghoff's asked him to feature us. WLS radio station says we are good Samaritans. Our principal announces our fame on LeMoyne's P.A. system.

Esther withdraws from the club. I don't know why. She moves to a different eighth grade room, too. Maybe she is being put into a different academic track?

***

I continue to see Esther because we are both in the confirmation class at Anshe Emet Synagogue. On Sunday mornings we have Sunday school led by Rabbi Solomon Goldman who teaches us about the stereotypes of Jews and anti-Semitism.

"There's no such thing as *looking* Jewish," Rabbi Goldman says. "Just look at Laurel. Small nose. Small chin."

"I take after my father," I say. "He's Gentile."

I look around the classroom. None of the other students catch my eye.

Rabbi Goldman scowls.

I scrunch down in my chair, in the back row.

Rabbi Goldman invites a Holocaust survivor to speak to our class. She is thin and frail but her voice commands the room. "Your mind is always free!" She scans the room, looks at me. "So you must never trust a Gentile."

Should I trust myself half the time?

"My father is a Gentile," I say. I trust him."

"Gentiles used the skin of little Jewish girls to make lampshades," says the Holocaust survivor.

The Associate Rabbi, Rabbi Schwartz teaches about the Jewish patriarchs. He passes back our exams in order of "worst" to "best" grade. I get mine back last. "You are one smart Jewish girl," Rabbi Schwartz says.

"Because I take after my father," I say.

"There are quotas for Jews in America's best universities," Dr. Stein, a pediatrician, tells our class.

I write a short story about a Jewish boy's rejection from medical school. A Jewish magazine publishes it. I win a prize. I am hopeful that it might help me fit in better at Anshe Emet. Maybe I could even get a best friend.

On Wednesday afternoons, like the Catholic children excused from school for their catechism class, Jewish children are excused for their confirmation class. The handsomest Rabbi ever, Rabbi Adelman teaches us. We sit in a semi-circle around him, and I hope that he notices me even though I don't look Jewish. We're using a spiral-bond, not-yet published workbook, *A Little Lower than the Angels*. There is a lot of up-to-date science findings for us to read followed by ample blank space to write our opinions on, for example, how the earth was formed, the idea of a God, and whether the Jewish people are the Chosen People, given the Holocaust. Rabbi Adelman doesn't check our work. He believes we have a "right to privacy." Esther is ecstatic because she figures she doesn't have to read or write. I'm relieved because I don't have to tell Esther what she thinks about what she hasn't read. After I leave home for college, my mother gives away all my books except for that workbook, even though I've written on the cover IF LOST, DO NOT RETURN.

On Friday nights, the confirmation class is supposed to attend Shabbat services. What some of us do is sign ourselves "in" and then go to the woman's lounge until the service is over when we can sign ourselves "out." I learn to smoke. Pall Malls.

I am in a stall when I hear Merle and Esther come into the lounge.

"What time will the party start?" Merle asks.

A party? Yeah! I am thinking.

"Eight O'clock," Esther says.

"Will it be in your ballroom?"

"Yes. We're having a live band for dancing."

Oh, yes! I am so excited.

"Who all is coming?"

"I've invited the entire confirmation class…"

What?

"…well, not quite the entire class. Not…you know…"

Doesn't Esther know that I might be in here?

***

Forty years pass and I am at my Senn High School reunion. Senn drew from fifteen grade schools, including mine, LeMoyne. I am wearing my best sheer black blouse and black Capri's, ready for the Friday night "kick-off" cocktail party.

"Laurie," a woman calls to me by my LeMoyne grade-school nickname, a nickname I abandoned decades ago. "I'd recognize you anywhere," she says. "Same small nose and small chin."

I smile at the woman I don't think I know.

"It's me," she says. "Esther!" She gives me a hug. "I was surprised to see your name on the list of attendees. But glad, too."

"I didn't recognize you," I say. Esther has transformed from a plain child into a stunning beauty. She looks like Audrey Hepburn. Cosmetic surgery has altered her nose, lifted her eyebrows, and nipped her chin. Cosmetics have given her luminous skin, contoured cheek bones and shimmering eyelids. Her beautician has straightened her hair, lightened it and given her a pixie cut. She is wearing a sleek three piece silk pant-suit, silver and black. Armani, I think. Her magenta nails blaze. She tells me she's a hostess at a Neiman-Marcus restaurant.

"Remember our *famous* rummage sale in your basement?" Esther asks.

"We were *so* famous," I say.

"My mother saw the newspaper stories about us. I told her that your father was Irish and your mother was Jewish but that it was a good marriage...they got on well."

Why would she have told her mother that?

"And their names were Tyrrell and Rose..."

Why would she remember their names?

"Esther! Hello!" a heavy-set woman with finely coiffed hair joins us. I vaguely recognize her as one of my confirmation classmates.

Coiffed glances at my nametag, nods, hugs Esther, and moves on.

"Hi, Eddie," Esther gives Eddie Edelson a big hug. He still has the bug eyes he had when he copied my spelling tests.

"Hi, Eddie," I say. He can't seem to place me.

"You're the first boy I kissed."

He slaps his forehead. "Oh, Laurie! You even look the same! Cute nose!"

"What are you doing now, Eddie?"

"I'm a lawyer."

"Gut Shabbos, Esther," says another well-dressed woman. And another. And another. They don't greet me.

"Let's catch up later," Esther says as she moves away in her same disjointed childhood walk. "Call me. Anytime. Room 303. Promise?"

"There you are! Laurie!" I turn and see a tall, gray-haired woman darting across the room. She's heavy-set, wearing a polyester pantsuit, sensible shoes, and a silver cross.

"Mary Anne McCoy," I say. I recognize her voice.

"I'd recognize you anywhere," she says. "You have the same face shape." She gives me a gentle hug. We talk about our lives and families like distant relatives at a family reunion, chatting without intimacy.

"Come over here, Linda." Mary Anne waves. "Here we are! Just us girls! JUGS!"

"Laurie, you look even more like Audrey Hepburn," Linda says.

"Laurie was our resident genius," Mary Anne says to her husband, Kurt, who has joined us. "The beauty and the brain."

"Join us for dinner, Laurie," Linda says.

"Thanks, but I am not hungry," I lie. The truth is that sadness has enveloped me, a sorrow I cannot identify.

"Join us tomorrow, then," Mary Anne says.

What I want to do tomorrow is to go to the Jewish cemetery where my grandparents are buried and put stones on their headstones. I've never been there. *Maybe there aren't any headstones?*

I wander back into the main room and sit next to Esther who is sitting next to her "best friend," Carol Cohen, a color-consultant, from California. She looks like spun platinum. She is thin, thin as a wand. She could be someone's fairy godmother.

Suzi Levine joins us. "Still such a cute nose," she says to me. She and Esther lift Carol up from the couch.

"Call anytime," Esther says, giving me a peck on the cheek. The three of them circle the main room where the Jews have congregated. Squeals, laughs, and happy hellos crescendo. Chicago nasal accents ascend from the ante-room where the Gentiles are hello-ing. I am exhausted.

***

"Please leave your phone message," says the hotel's computerized voice mail.

"Esther, I am going to breakfast, now. Here's my cell-phone number."

***

"Join us," Mary Anne says. She and Kurt are eating bacon and eggs.

"No, thanks," I lie "I have to call my husband."

I go to my room, phone home. Phone Esther. Same computerized message. Call best friend, Betty. Call Esther. Same message. Call Waldheim Cemetery. No Calls Answered on Sabbath. Call Esther. Same message. I am not sure why I keep phoning Esther. I go back down to the lobby. Mary Anne, Kurt and Linda are there.

"Join us," Mary Anne says. "We're going on a field trip to LeMoyne."

The cemetery doesn't accept phone calls on Shabbat so I can't find out where my grandparents graves are located, and Esther is unavailable, so I squeeze into the backseat of a two door sedan, happy to be out of the hotel and away from my deepening sadness.

Kurt drives us south to Addison Avenue. Now, sculptures mark the corners. LeMoyne's play equipment is gone and the school yard's cemented over. It is a "Six Dollar a Spot" parking lot, advertised in English and Spanish.

"My parents owned that building," I say, pointing to a graystone three story. "We lived on the top floor. I baby-sat for tenants."

Kurt stops the car. The building is for sale for seven figures.

"You must have been rich," Kurt says.

"Oh, in the middle," I say.

We turn up Cornelia.

"Oh, no! Our rummage sale building is gone!" Linda says. The brick six-flat my family owned and lived in has been demolished, replaced by a contemporary glass and steel eye-sore.

Kurt drives east to Lake Shore Drive and turns north,

"That's where Esther lived," I say pointing to the corner highrise. "On the nineteenth floor…And Eddie lived in that next building… and Merle there, too." I silently name more children to myself who lived in these high rises on the Drive. I realize that all these rich kids were Jewish.

As we continue driving north, I do not ask to be driven past Anshe Emet. *By not playing my Jewish card, am I by default playing my Gentile one? I don't like this card-game!*

***

Saturday night dinner. Jews and Gentiles are sitting in different parts of the dining room. *Where should I sit?*

"I'm sorry, there's no room at our table," Mary Anne says, "but we've saved you a seat at the next table."

"There you are," Morris Greenblatt says. "You are still such a cute thing."

"Here comes your wife, Morris," I say, pushing his hands off me just as I always had.Esther saunters over in a bespoke black lace and silk mid-calf gown. She says, "I...blah, blah, blah...But I've got your cell phone number now, Laurie." She returns to her table. She signals a waiter to remove the one empty chair.

"LeMoyne Grade School picture now being taken," the photographer announces. "Wait," I shout. "Where's Esther?" I get her. "Merle?" I get her, too. I round up Suzi, Linda, and Mary Anne. I am an eighth grader again, the leader of my classmates, organizing them, nicely ordering them around, taking charge of their lives, integrating them, Jews and Gentiles posed together. *My life's purpose? My destiny?*

* * *

A corner of the hotel's restaurant has been designated "SUNDAY BRUNCH FOR REUNION GUESTS ONLY."

"Join us," Linda says. She's sitting in what must be the unofficially designated Gentile area.

"Sit here, instead," Esther says, pointing to a chair at her table. Carol, Merle and Suzi are there. Esther's dressed down, wearing linen.

"I need to talk to Esther," I tell Linda as I join Esther's table.

I can't stand it another minute. I decide to take a risk and say, "Esther this Jewish-Gentile split is driving me crazy. I'm about to explode."

"Well, now that you mention it," Esther says, "we were talking about you last night."

"We?"

"We went out after dinner, and we were talking about you," Esther repeats.

"We?" I ask again.

"I always felt sorry for you," Esther continues. I don't see pity in her eyes.

"What?" *No one has ever said anything like that to me.*

"We talked about how you're being half-Jewish is like being half-Black now. Back then, Jews couldn't accept you and neither could the Gentiles. But I told them last night how you rose above it. Look how you've pulled yourself up."

Breathe Laurel breathe. What is she talking about? Pulled myself up from what? Not being accepted by a group of twelve year olds?

"I always felt sorry for you because you looked so Gentile."

My anger rises as I look at her pseudo-Gentile surgically altered nose and chin. Lightened hair. Straightened. She looks like me. My mind flits to seeing my mother on the phone, looking grim. After hanging up, she tells me I have been dis-invited to Eddie Edelman's Bar Mitzvah party. I feel she thinks it is my fault.

Esther continues, "My mother talked to the Sisterhood about you and they agreed that you should not be included in the confirmation party. They saw your picture in the paper. And, you know, your name, *Richardson.*"

I am speechless. *Who talks like this? Thinks like this?*

"Call me when you're in Chicago, again," Esther says, getting up from her chair. Her nails blazing.

I am baffled about Esther. Can she possibly have been acting out of a multi-decade grudge towards me for being "too cute" and "too smart"? Should I even think this let alone write it? Do I really think it's all about me?

Why should I have cared enough about her to keep phoning and getting dissed, taking it?

So that I won't feel split?

Missing half of myself?

CHAPTER 9

MARIA

"Princess-and-the-pea!" That's Father's name for me when I complain that my bed hurts me.

"My thighs. Calves. Even behind my knees," I moan. I have woken up from the pain and stumbled into the kitchen.

"You're having what's called *growing* pains, " Father says.

I am surprised he has used the word, "pain." He doesn't believe in pain.

"Will they stop?" I ask. I squeeze my right thigh, the one that hurts the most.

"Yes, if you stop *thinking* about them. Oh, and, watch how Kitty stretches. Copy her."

Over the summer that I turn twelve I grow six-inches. When eighth grade starts, I am five-foot-ten inches and one-hundred and two pounds. I am taller than my mother, sister, and all the boys and girls in my class. Except for one girl, Maria Martinez. She and I are the same height but she weighs more. She is curvy with hips and breasts while I look like a knitting needle.

My mother is our Room Mother. She visits each child's home trying to get other mothers to help in our classroom's parties and field-trips. Mother tells me to become "best friends" with Maria.

"Why?" I ask

"Because I say so," Mother says.

I am reticent. Maria is too shy and walks too slowly. She isn't very pretty. Plus, I am grieving the loss of my last best friend, Valerie, and trying to figure out if the new girl, Esther, could be my new best friend.

Father is rarely home for the week-day suppers Mother serves at five o'clock sharp. Barrie usually arrives at 4:59. Jessica is in college.

"Invite Maria over after school," Mother insists. "Invite her to stay for supper."

"Why?"

"Because I want you to."

***

"That's rhubarb," Mother explains. Maria helps herself to the entire serving dish. Mother does not stop her or correct her.

"Invite her again," Mother says.

"Why?"

"Because."

***

"That's breaded veal," Mother explains. "They are small. Take several—take more." Maria takes four cutlets, leaving one each for Mother, Barrie and me. Barrie makes a squirrely face, but Mother stops him from making a snarky comment. I am happy to see someone being "a good eater," something I have never been and am routinely scolded about. I really don't like much food or much of it and if the food is gone Mother can't be on me to "eat!" Maybe, having Maria as a new best-friend is a good idea.

Maria comes to my house twice a week after school and stays for supper. Mother always wishes her a special good-bye in the kitchen. Maybe, mother is explaining to her about different kinds of food. Maybe, Mother needs to because Maria is not Jewish. She's Catholic.

"That's beef brisket."

"That's challah—bread."

"That's potato pancakes."

"That's green apple pie."

I am relieved not to have to eat much of any of it. I am especially relieved when we don't have leftovers. Especially the awful pies Mother makes every day for Barrie.

"I think you should visit Maria in her apartment," Mother says.

"Why?"

"Because then the friendship is more equal…Oh, and take this package with you."

***

Maria and I walk down Addison Avenue past the El and Cubs Park. It is the farthest west that I have ever walked. She lives in a two-room basement apartment with a narrow kitchen. Mrs. Martinez looks so young and so sad. She sleeps in the bedroom with Maria's baby sister, Rosalie. Maria sleeps on a green folding sofa in the main room beneath a wall crucifix.

"Mother asked me to give you this," I say to Mrs. Martinez, handing her the package.

Mother has knit blankets, jackets and hats in the same multi-colored wool she has used for knitting my sweaters. Mrs. Martinez tries to thank me, but she is crying too hard, and then Rosalie is crying, too.

Maria and I get into a once-a-week rhythm in her apartment. We settle on the green sofa. Mrs. Martinez sets up a card-table in front of us, facing away from the wall, and I am glad that the Jesus crucifix is not in my sight-line. I am not sure if I am being sacrilegious as a half-Jewish girl for sitting beneath Jesus' body, but I don't think my mother would see a problem as she has been here herself.

On the table are envelopes, pens, and pages of people's names and addresses. Maria and I begin addressing the envelopes.

"Write legibly," Mrs. Martinez says. "We get paid by the envelope."

"How much?" I ask.

"A penny an envelope."

"What's this?" I ask. The table has been layered with magazines.

"Find and cut out coupons," Mrs. Martinez instructs us. "We can sell the ones we can't use."

***

"How do you like being at Maria's house?" Mother asks me. I am holding a hank of multi-colored yarn between my outstretched hands as mother winds it into a ball so it won't get tangled when she knits.

"I do like it," I say. I spread my hands further apart, and my heart seems to expand, too. "I like being helpful."

"Thank you for helping me, now," Mother says. She drops the new ball of yarn into the basket at her feet.   .

"I like playing with the baby Rosalie, too," I say. I stretch out my arms out in front of me, hands folded back at my wrists. I twist at my waist.

"You are growing, Laurel."

"Without any pain!" I raise my shoulders toward my ears.

Mother picks up a shopping bag and says, "Take this to Baby Rosalie. She's growing, too."

I peak inside the bag and see a sweater in the same multi-colored wool that I am wearing. I like that we have matching sweaters.

Maria and I graduate from Le Moyne Elementary School. Maria wins a scholarship to Resurrection High School for Girls, and I go to Senn High. We go our separate ways.

***

Twenty years later, I am in a café line at Chicago's Art Institute when I hear my name called.

"Laurie...It's me, Maria."

Maria's shiny hair is pulled back into a pony-tail, her cheeks are rosy, and her eyes sparkle. *I wonder if she is pregnant. She has that glow.*

We hug.

"I didn't recognize you," I say.

"You haven't changed at all," she says.

"Thanks...I guess."

"Let's eat lunch," Maria says. "Catch up."

We settle on a table near the ersatz waterfall. I have tuna-salad and coffee. Maria has the lunch special, turkey and all the trimmings.

"Looks like you're still a little eater," Maria says.

"And you're still a big one," I say.

"I'm eating for three." Maria pats her stomach. "Twins coming."

"Lucky you!" I say." "No twins for me—but I have two sons—four years apart."

"I have three more at home," Maria says. "My husband comes from a big Catholic family and we both love children."

"Of course. Who wouldn't after living with your little sister, Rosalie? How is she?"

Maria puts down her fork. "You didn't know, did you?"

"Didn't know what?"

"Rosalie wasn't my sister. She was my niece."

I try to get my mind around what she is telling me.

"The woman you knew as Mrs. Martinez wasn't my mother. She was my sister. *Miss* Martinez. My father and my mother were both dead. My sister had custody of me."

"My mother knew all of this?"

"She had been to our apartment. She knew we were poor. That's why she sent food back with me."

"I didn't know she did that. She never said anything."

"Your mother was humble."

"She loved hearing about Maria."

"Your mother was so good-hearted. She didn't judge my sister."

Then it finally hits me. Maria's sister was an *unwed mother*.

In the Forties—when Rosalie was born—the shame and stigma of being an unwed mother was unrelenting. An unmarried pregnant daughter "went away" to live in a maternity home. If she went to a Catholic home, she would likely be considered a sinner and a neurotic unable to control her sexual impulses, and, therefore, unfit to be an actual mother. Only if the girl acknowledged her shame and guilt could she possibly have a chance for a "normal" life, a home and family. And, the only *real* way to acknowledge her guilt was to "give up" the child. This is the price she has to pay for her sinfulness. Her baby joins what was popularly called "the baby scoop," where maternity homes acted as "breeding agents" for adoptive parents.

"An unwed mother who kept her baby," I say.

"Yes. She believed abortion or suicide were mortal sins—out of the question."

My mind jumps to 1954. I am in college. My best friend is pregnant. She doesn't tell her boyfriend. She doesn't want children. She has found an abortionist. I lend her $300. We take a taxi to a high-rise building on Chicago's north side. I wait for her. We take a taxi back. I stay with her. We never talk about it again. I feel complicit. She does not repay my loan.

1955. My father says he knows of a very *well-bred* baby that my sister could adopt. He can vouch for the parents. Do I think he should raise the issue with my sister? I do. He does. Her husband rejects the idea. He does not want to adopt a baby from an "unwed mother."

I have forgotten whatever else went on in that conversation, but I remember that Father and I are alone, sitting on the leather couch at our lake house. I remember that at the conclusion of our conversation, I decide that should I ever become pregnant without being married, I would commit suicide.

"Your sister was very brave," I say to Maria. "I admire her."

We hug, exchange addresses and promise to keep in touch.

My opinion of my mother goes up. She acted not only with kindness toward Maria and her family, she acted in gentle defiance of the culture.

Why? Perhaps she had had some growing pains, too? Perhaps taking care of baby Rosemary gave my mother a peace that until then had eluded her.

CHAPTER 10

SOUL-MATE: NATHALIE

"Here," Nathalie says. She's dramatically holding a book of poems to her heart. "You'll see what I mean." Her cheeks are flushed. "Look! Here!"

She hands me the book. I am confused. The poet has violated every grammatical and punctuation rule I have ever learned. No words are capitalized, simple words are combined to create new ones, "am," "if" and "because" have become nouns, and the spacing between words, lines and stanzas is eccentric. Then, my cheeks are flushing, too. I don't understand much of the content—it seems private and some of it rather erotic—but oh my how my visual, tactile and aural senses have been aroused, mixed together. Sounds have colors.

"Fab!" I say. "Maybe we can write any way we want to."

Nathalie grins. She tilts her head. She looks like the Cheshire cat with her soft blond hair and hazel eyes. She strokes the crucifix on the chain around her neck and slides it idly from breast bone to breast bone. I stroke my left wrist. We each have a hand-habit that comforts, grounds us, and reminds us that we are alive.

Nathalie and I met as Senn High School freshmen in advanced English. The class met just before our lunch hour. Although we belong to different sororities and are each expected to eat lunch with our sisters, we decide to hang out with each other at *The Penguin* where we could talk, drink coffee and smoke Pall Malls. We are thirteen. We think of ourselves as *literati* renegades and now we have fallen-in-love with e.e.cummings.

"Did you bring your notebook?" Nathalie asks.

"Of course…Did you?"

"Of course…Do you want to go first?"

"Why don't you?"

We have this writing game. One of us writes the first line of a poem, reads it aloud with dramatic high-notes or whispery voice, as

© KONINKLIJKE BRILL NV, LEIDEN, 2019 | DOI:10.1163/9789004411364_010

required. The other listens, enrapt—or at least giving the appearance of same—and then, after a bit of time the other one writes the next line of the poem, reading it aloud with feeling and so on and so on until the two-authored, integrated, stageable poem is complete. Often, we don't know who has written what.

But, now, with the discovery of e.e.cummings all our writing transgressions feel passé. Can we write in a cummingsing way *together*? We try.

<pre>
          my   you

       y(our)   m[i]ne

   once   a   pon

          an
                    [if]
</pre>

"Why aren't you taking Latin?" I ask Nathalie. "We could study that together, too."

" I am half French," she answers. "So I take French."

"That makes no sense."

"Oh, but it does make sense," Nathalie says, smiling. "Easy A."

Three years earlier a junior high-school teacher had told my parents that I "talked too fast." "Probably," she informed them, because my "brain was going faster than my mouth." *Duh! Whose brain doesn't?* Father thought I talked too loudly. "A soft voice is becoming in a woman," he told me, even though I was still a child. To solve these putative speech problems, Father enrolled me in elocution lessons at the Goodman Theater in downtown Chicago. Three years later, I am a member of the Junior Theater Troupe.

"Nathalie," I insist, "Come on, take acting lessons at the Goodman. Try-out for the Troupe." She did and she did.

On Saturdays we take the Lake Shore Drive bus downtown for our Junior Acting Class. We take turns sitting by the window, over the rear tire, where the bumps are the best.

"She sells seashells by the sea shore." We practice our sibilants together, getting louder and louder and faster and faster.

"Around the rugged rock the ragged rascals ran." We are revved up.

"Toy boat. Toy boat. Toy boat." Giggles.

"Eleven benevolent elephants."

"Twelve twins twice twist twine."

By the time we go through the repertoire of our tongue-twisting duologues our sides are hurting from laughter and our lipstick's licked off by our twisting-tongues.

"Do I look okay?" I ask after re-applying Revlon's *Pink Storm* to my lower lip and smacking it against my upper one. She nods. She applies *Pink Storm* and smacks her lips. I nod. We don't need mirrors. We have each other. We are each other.

My face is a curious one. I have my Russian mother's high cheekbones, upturned nose and small chin, and my father's wide-set Irish eyes and brownish-red hair. I look exotic. My legs are long, my head small and round. I am hipless and breastless, shaped rather like a ruler. Nathalie's oval face is perfectly symmetrical, her skin porcelain-like. Her head is in perfect proportion to her body's average height, weight, and shapeliness. She is neither too big nor too small.

"Just right!" Madame Prokioff says when appraising Nathalie for any ingénue part in any play. Nathalie is a director's dream-child, a Galatea for a Pygmalion, a graceful chameleon. She knows it, too, emphasizing the blank canvas of herself by dressing only in beige. I wear red. Madame casts me as the evil stepmother—teacher, witch, giantess.

Nathalie and I are as serious on the bus ride back home as we are silly on the way out. We compulsively practice our lines, learning each other's, too. I am never jealous of her central role because it is as if I have two parts, hers and mine.

"See you later, alligator," one of us says when we part.

"After a while, crocodile," the other responds.

"Later."

"Gator."

"While."

"Dile."

"Call me!" We shout in unison.

***

We turn fourteen. I am having my first overnight at Nathalie's. I think myself extraordinarily lucky to have found my *soul-mate*. She lives in a small apartment in a large apartment complex near our high school. What should be the dining room is Nathalie's bedroom. We stretch out on her bed, sip Chartreuse and smoke the Gauloises her French mother leaves for us so we'll be occupied while she entertains some man in the back bedroom.

"Il n'y a pas de quoi," Nathalie says, nose raised up high, shoulder shrugged and hands waving toward the back bedroom. She translates for me, "It does not matter."

"Does anything?" I ask. I scan her bookshelf.

We have immersed ourselves in the French existentialists and questions of human existence—*Being and Nothingness*—English translation.

"How can we know how to live our lives when nothing matters more than anything else." Nat asks. She looks glum.

"We can choose our own life, though," I say. "Choose how to live it."

"And how to leave it, too," Nat says. She fiddles with her cross.

"Look at all our freedoms," I say, sipping my Chartreuse.

"What about God, then?" Nat looks pained. "Does God have anything to say about it?"

"C'mon Nat," I say. "You know that our knowledge is always fallible and limited. You know we invented a God to give us certainty." I had learned this in my confirmation class at Anshe Emet Synagogue. Anshe Emet? *Men of Truth.*

"So, it's all up to me? No God. No givens. Nothing." Nat twists the lace on her sleeping gown. She is agitated. "So, I get to choose to be or not-to-be, to act or not-to-act."

"Yes. I think that's how it is."

"And the way I act is who I am. I *act* myself into Being." She slips off her gold chain and cross and lets them slip to the floor. "When moments of decision come, it is my responsibility—mine alone—to act purposively. Oui?"

"Yeah."

"What a terrible burden!"

"Mes petites filles!" Nathalie's mother is in our room. "Why are you up so late? Ah, I see you found the Chartreuse…Is it not so pretty?…Did it not taste so good?…Did it not make you want to go to sleep?" She is pretty. She looks young enough to be Nathalie's sister. "Mon Dieu," she says picking up Nathalie's cross. Her naked body is visible under her sheer-silken robe.

"Hello!" A tall thin man is at our door. His hat is in his hands. I pull a blanket up around me. He smiles at Nathalie. "How are you tonight, little lady? Just lookie at you…Growing up so much."

"Au revoir, Neil," Nathalie's mother says. She dangles the little cross in front of her breasts.

"Your money's in the envelope on the kitchen table," Neil says. "As usual."

I wince, audibly.

"See you next week," Neil calls back, as he's walked down the hallway.

"Who are *you* to judge?" Nathalie says.

She has never talked that way to me before.

As I write this now I wonder if Neil was Nathalie's father.

***

"Maman est morte." Tears stream down Nathalie's face. Groans of despair escape from her twisted-up mouth. She is shivering, her breathing labored, her hands shaky. She pulls on her hair and screams.

"What?" I say. "You know I don't understand French."

"My mother died today," she says. Her tears have stopped, shivers gone, breathing normal, voice normal. She grins.

"What?"

"It's the first line of *The Stranger*," she says.

"What?"

"Camus's *magnifique roman. J'l'adore.* I love it. *Très existential!* I am going to use it for an *ingénue* try-out."

"So, *your* mother is *not* dead?"

"*No, mon ami.* I am just practicing."

I don't know if I am angrier over her French, her theatrics or her toying with my capacity for empathy.

"But, I really should speak Camus's words with no emotion. None." Nat's face goes blank.

"What are you talking about?" I yawn. I can feign no feelings, too.

"Mersault—the main character of the novel expresses no grief at his mother's funeral, refuses to look at her dead body and then goes off and has sex."

"Sounds like a jerk," I say.

"Later, he kills a man for no particular reason, shows no remorse and is sentenced to be guillotined."

"Serves him right," I say. I decide to play along although I don't believe in the death penalty.

"While in jail, Mersault rages at the meaninglessness of existence and he rages against people who have judged him for who he is."

"I'd have been one of the ragers."

"But then Mersault comes to terms with his forthcoming execution." She opens *The Stranger*. "Here. Listen to this." She reads in English the last lines of the novel:

"I opened myself to the benign indifference of the world. Finding it so much like myself——I felt that I had been happy and to wish that there be a large crowd of spectators the day of my execution and that they greet me with cries of hate."

"It's beautiful writing," I say. "But I don't accept the ideas."

"I do," she says.

***

We come from the movie, *Moulin Rouge,* to our hang-out, the *Uptown Grill.* We suck ketchup off French fries, sip chocolate malts and take drags off our fags. Bright red lipstick stains her Gauloises, light pink stains my Pall Malls. She wears mascara, eye-shadow and rouge. I am not permitted to "gild the lily." She wears a black turtleneck. I wear a pink cashmere sweater set.

"Jose Ferrar," she trembles while saying the movie star's name. "*Mon bel homme!*"

"What?" I counter. "He's ugly and tiresome. And old!"

We argue. She is obsessed with all things French and existential. I don't like French anything, anymore. Is our friendship being destroyed over this difference? Or, are we arguing on purpose to make our forthcoming separation easier?

We are fifteen. Nathalie plans to finish high school in two more years, get a scholarship to Northwestern University and major in theater. She basks in the idea of being an ingénue forever. I am matriculating at the University of Chicago in two weeks. At the close of our sophomore year, I will no longer be a high-schooler. I will be a college freshman.

***

My parents move to the countryside. I join the University Theater and *Compass Players,* the precursor to *Second City.* I love our improvisational work but my theatrical interests turn to performances in real-life, such as sitting in at Walgreen's counter to help racially integrate it, testing landlords' discriminatory renting policies, chaining myself to Frank Lloyd Wright's *Robie House* to prevent its scheduled demise. My day-to-day life revolves around social activism, friends, and my graduate student boyfriend. During vacations, I go to New York City. I live there in the summer, working as a key-punch operator. I never again return to my north side neighborhood. I never again see Nathalie.

***

I can still see, though, our last time together. We are sitting across from each other at a round table at the *Uptown Grill*, her hazel eyes unsmiling. We have exhausted ourselves arguing over things French.

"Pour toi," Nathalie says, handing me a little box. Inside is an enameled peacock-blue Lady Ronson cigarette lighter, engraved: To L.R. from N.H.

"Mur-see-ber-coo," I say in my absurd French accent, trying to sound conciliatory. I thumb click the lighter's clicker to no avail.

"Tu must get *le fluide!*" Nathalie takes a dime out of her wallet, unscrews a little screw on the bottom of the lighter, makes a grand swooping gesture with her right hand towards the space she has created in my lighter, and declares, *"Le fluide ici."*

That was the last word I remember Nathalie saying to me: *Here*.

***

I use that lighter until I lose it, but I don't remember when or where. I must have felt the loss, but I cannot recover that feeling. Nathalie's and my universities were only sixty miles apart geographically but star-distances apart academically and politically. I move on in my life. I assume she does, too. From time to time, I check television and theater cast-lists, looking for her name. I wonder if she tries to find me.

"Has anyone heard from Nathalie?" I ask at Senn High School's fiftieth reunion.

"Don't you know, Laurie," Leanne says.

"Know what?"

"She died."

I try to get my mind around my *soul-mate* having died.

"Of what?" I ask.

"Suicide." Leanne says.

"Oh, no! How? When?"

Leanne clears her throat and tells the story. After Nathalie's first year in college, she went to a festival in Santa Fe. There, she met and fell in love with a Navajo, got pregnant, dropped out of college and moved into his Hogan on the reservation. After their son's birth, the man became abusive. Natalie wanted to leave the reservation but she could not legally take her son with her. Her drinking problem intensified. One morning before the sun came up, she decided to take her bottle of gin for a walk along the train tracks. The train came on schedule. She was nineteen.

When I hear the news, I feel sorrow and loss, but mostly I am disturbed that I had not known that Nathalie was dead—not that I would have learned about it through a letter or something tangible but I should have known through my intuition.

Maybe I had the intuition and ignored it, the same way I ignored losing the Lady Ronson lighter she had given me. Maybe I lost the lighter at the same moment she lost her life?

Although over sixty years have passed since our separation, as I write this I am in a rage. Surely, Natalie had read Camus's *Myth of Sisyphus*—probably in French. Had she not understood Camus? Even if there are no eternal values and no meaning in the world, suicide is never okay. Never. Even nihilism cannot condone taking one's own life. One must always go on living and creating no matter how desolate one feels. *Nathalie, you shouldn't have done it.*

Nat, I felt desolated, powerless and hopeless, too, when I was nineteen. Many nineteen year olds do, you know. Oh, Nat! Damn You!! Ingénue! Why didn't you shout out the lines from Samuel Beckett's *The Unnamable?* "*I can't go on. I'll go on.*"

I realize as I write about Nathalie H. how central she has been to the shaping of my life. With Nathalie beside me, both of us barely in our teens, I set upon what have become mainstays of my life—writing, performing, and studying the meaning of meaning.

In writing about her, she comes alive to me—*in me*. She goes on. A soul-mate. *Ici.* Here.

PART 3
FAMILY TIES

Once a twin, always a twin.

Anon

COUSIN KATIE

"I'm dying, Laurel." No *hello*. Just, "I'm dying."

"What?" I say. Two decades have passed since I have spoken to my age-mate cousin, Katie. I have no idea why I feel compelled to phone her this afternoon.

I am not sure if I can write this.

"Cancer's gone into my brain," Katie tells me. "Doc just told me that there was nothing more he could do for me."

"I'll come," I say. It is May, 2001. I am surprised at my immediate and unconditional willingness to uproot my life in Columbus to be with my dying cousin in New York City. We have been in-and-out of each other's lives over our years but mostly out. Now, I can't fathom letting her go—die—without spending time with her, being with her, my one and only age-mate cousin.

It will be easier if I begin with family history and when Katie and I first met.

In 1908, our Jewish Gramma escaped the pogroms in Russia and came to America. *I can't seem to write that often enough.* She brought with her young children—Mike, Rose, and Ceil. Mike met my father, Tyrrell, in Bughouse Square, a place of free-speech in Chicago. Mike was a Communist and Tyrrell a Republican, a law student. They were taken with each other's cleverness. Mike invited Tyrrell to board with his Jewish family. Tyrrell was the first Gentile to cross Gramma's threshold.

When Tyrrell and Rose, my mother, fell in love and married, Gramma had a nervous breakdown. Father promised to raise her grandchildren Jewish. Gramma recovered and her three grandchildren—Jessica, Barrie and me—were raised Jewish. Well, except during the summer when we went to Christian Family Camp,

© KONINKLIJKE BRILL NV, LEIDEN, 2019 | DOI:10.1163/9789004411364_011

which was my Mother's idea. She did not want her children to suffer, as she had, for being Jewish, although she never told us that in words. Deeds speak loud.

Before I was born, Uncle Mike had moved to Los Angeles following some major rift between him and the Chicago family. So deep was the chasm that I didn't know I had an Uncle Mike or a cousin Katie until the Passover when Uncle Mike and cousin Katie came to Chicago. Katie and I were both seven.

I had been "the baby" in my family's circles and I could have been jealous about Katie sharing my special place. But I was not jealous. I was intrigued, fascinated.

Katie seems to glide from room-to-room rather than walk. Her arms seem to float weightlessly when she raises them. Her black hair smells of lavender. She is smaller than me with thin little bones. She wears ballet slippers instead of Buster Brown's. Her over-dress is gossamer sheer, the under-one a deep pink. Store bought. I wear a red and blue plaid vest and skirt. Homemade. Katie's blue-eyes are barely visible behind her thick glasses and her nose is quite large. I feel protective of her, maybe even a little bit in love with her in a slightly bigger sister way.

Aunt Ceil seats herself at the Passover table next to her brother, Uncle Mike. She seats Katie between Barrie and me.

"What's Passover?" Katie whispers to me. Her whispery voice sounds like mine.

"It's when God passed over all the Jewish houses and didn't kill their first-born sons dead like he did the Egyptian ones," I whisper back.

"God?" she whispers through a smirky smile.

"That's why God won't kill my awful brother." I point a celery stick toward Barrie.

Uncle Mike points a carrot stick towards Katie.

"Barrie's a magician," I whisper to Katie.

"Maybe you could make my father disappear?" Katie whispers to Barrie. She waves a celery stick at him He waves one back.

I don't know if Katie is an ally in my battles with Barrie or if they are trying to entice each other.

"I could," Barrie says. "But I won't tonight. Instead, watch this." Barrie shows Katie a coin in the palm of his hand. He makes a fist, opens it and the coin is gone. "Where is it?" he asks.

Katie shakes her head.

"Here it is," he says, taking the coin from behind her ear.

Jampa raises his wine glass and talks in Hebrew.

"Drink your wine, Katie." I say "Like this." I chug down my little serving.

Katie tastes hers and then chugs it down, too. She slyly smiles.

"Can we have more?" she asks me.

"Not yet," I say.

Barrie passes a stick of Juicy Fruit to Katie.

Jampa breaks off a piece of matzah, wraps it in a napkin and leaves the room.

"I know where he's hidden it," I tell Katie.

"What?"

"It's a little game," I say. "Jampa needs that piece of matzah to finish the Seder."

"Will Barrie find it behind my ear?" she asks, laughing. Hoping?

"How is this night different from all other nights?" Jampa asks in English. Around the world, the youngest person at the Passover table answers that question. Katie is almost asleep from wine and hunger and I doubt she knows the answer, anyway, so I show-off for my family and for Katie by answering, "Tonight we eat matzah... unleavened bread." But what I want to say is that this night is different because I am meeting my only age-mate cousin, Katie. I like her and she likes me.

"Passover is all about *freedom,*" Uncle Mike is saying. "It is not about Jews and Egyptians. It is about freedom *from* rich people oppressing the poor and freedom *from* the tyranny of private property and freedom for the workers to unite and for the opium of the people to..."

Katie rolls her eyes, rhythmically taps the table and chews her Juicy Fruit, open-mouthed.

Barrie rolls his eyes, too, and hands Katie another stick of gum.

"Dayenu!" Gramma shouts. "Enough!"

"Not now, Mike," Father says.

Katie makes a victory "V" with her fingers.

"What's this?" Barrrie says, "finding" a coin on Katie's shoulder.

"Ess Gesunt!" Mother says.

"We can eat our supper, now," I translate for Katie.

Mother puts a platter of roast chicken on the table.

Aunt Ceil puts a wing on Katie's plate.

"I don't eat birds," Katie whispers.

"Pretend," I say.

"Can I drink some more wine?" she asks

"*Ken*," I say "Yes."

Barrie pours wine up to the rim of Katie's wine glass. Then, he moves his hand around the rim of her water glass until it yields a sweet vibrating tone. Katie hip-sways in her chair, chugs the wine.

"Kindele, Leah and Katie," Jampa says. "You are both the youngest so together you must find the hidden matzah?"

"Open that drawer," I say to Katie, pointing to the sofa's end-table.

"I found it," she shouts. "*I* found it."

I let her claim the victory.

"I mean *we* found it," she shouts even more loudly.

I think Katie changing the "I" to "we" in our moment of Seder triumph makes all the difference. I was ready to give the glory to Katie but she declared us a twosome. *We* had brought together the broken piece of matzah, symbolically bringing our broken family together. Katie and I together did it, the two of us made a whole.

We become pen-pals...until we aren't...

For the next years, although we do not see each other—or maybe because we don't—we become pen-pals. I have saved and re-read our letters through multiple moves over the decades. My letters to her are still legible copies on onion skin. At first we write little-nothings in our best print. I ask about Uncle Mike, she asks about Barrie. By the time we are efficient writers in cursive, our letters grow longer and more revelatory.

When we are twelve, I write I am sad because my best friend, Valerie, is moving to the country. Katie responds that she has never had a friend because "all the girls are jealous of how well I dance." I tell her "not to tell anyone but that I had my first kiss at Joan's party...we were playing post office and Eddie sent me a special-delivery letter." She replies, "I don't go to parties so I don't know what playing post-office means. It sounds a little childish, if you don't mind me saying so. I don't need a party to kiss a boy!" I tell her I had lent my paper on the Chicago fire to Sandra and Sandra copied it word-for-word and told Miss West that I was the copier. My lawyer father came to school, defended me and proved my case. I write Katie, "I feel shaky ever since discovering that some people just plain lie. Even lie right to my face."

Approaching thirteen, our correspondence takes an uneasy turn:

Dear Cousin-Laurel

Send me some of your papers so I can hand them in. I am dancing all the time now.

My mother is back in the looney-bin. She gets so bad before she goes in. This time she threatened me with a kitchen knife. Don't tell anyone, especially not my father. I am afraid child services will take me away between my mother's nuttiness and my father's stupid politics. You are so lucky!

I wish I were you!!

XOXOXOXOX0
Cousin-K.

Dear Cousin-K,

I wrote a story about a Jewish boy who couldn't get into medical school because of the quotas. It won a prize in a Jewish magazine. It's called, "NOT WANTED!"

Do you want a copy? You can use it if you want.

Love and hugs,
Laurel

Dear Laurel,

I can dance like Salome. (HA!) Don't bother to send the story you wrote. I think I already saw the movie. (Ha-ha!)

XXXX
K.

When Katie and I turn thirteen, Katie writes that she is "trying out sex…faking orgasms on the front porch so that her father could hear." She describes her mother as "a Zombie when she isn't a Vampire."

"I know things about you, that you don't know," she writes. "Things my father told me but I can't tell you. I can't tell anyone."

"Was I adopted?" I write back.

"Worse. But I can't tell you. Ha! Ha!"

"TELL ME!"

"No. Oh, and I have decided to change my name. From now on my name is *Laurel*—just like yours."

"You cannot do that," I write back, furious. "You cannot take my name. *Kine hora!* Gramma says that if you take the name of someone who is living that means you wish that person dead."

"I don't wish *you* dead," Katie writes back. "So, I will only change my name to *Laura*. I am not quite you. I am Laura."

Katie and I meet again…college…

When my junior year at the University of Chicago begins, Katie decides to transfer from Mills College (probably the best dance program in the country) to the University of Wisconsin so she can, as she puts it, "reunite" with me.

About once a month she takes the train from Madison to Chicago and crashes on the living-room couch in the apartment I share with Maggie, a dancer. Katie has had a nose-job. What once was large is now small and upturned. "Just like yours, Laurel," Katie says showing off her profile. She wears her hair in a pony-tail with bangs. Just like mine. Her blue eyes are now brown, like mine. "Contacts," she tells me. "They come in colors, now." I wear no make-up. She, too, is bare-faced. She visits without a suitcase so she can rummage through my closet. "Black and brown stripes, Laurel. Your favorite. Mine, too." Having to roll up the sleeves and pant-legs amuses her. "I am just a smaller version of you," she says, her hands dancing my shape. She convinces my friends to call her "Laura," choreographs dances for Maggie and herself and performs them for my theater friends. She enchants them with claims that she personally knows the Hollywood Ten, the film people accused of being communists. She eats my stash of gourmet jelly beans. "Free love is the only love," she says. She sleeps with my boyfriend!

Katie and I go our separate ways.

For the next five years or so Katie and I learn of each other through our Aunt Ceil. Katie goes to New York City and founds the Laura Foreman Dance Company at the New School of Social Research. I earn my doctorate in sociology, marry a fellow graduate student, a mathematician named Herb, and we have a son, Benjamin. Herb receives a teaching position at Harvey Mudd College in Claremont, California. I stay home for six-months to take care of Benjamin and make curtains, until I start climbing them. I secure a position at California State University-Los Angeles. I think nothing new will ever happen for me. I am twenty-six years old. So is Katie.

To my pre-marriage eyes, Herb was a combo of James Dean, Rene Descartes and Nature Boy—a very very smart free spirit who knew how to survive anything and everything. He knew what plants and insects were edible, how to make water potable, start a flint-fire, catch, clean and pit-fry fish, rabbits and tortoises, should any of this become necessary. And it might because we were graduate students at the University of Colorado-Boulder, just south of the nuclear weapons facility at Rocky Flats. Eye-witness accounts report that a fire in the plutonium processing building had not been completely contained but that plumes of radioactive smoke had drifted over Boulder. Firefighters eventually extinguished the fire with water thereby exposing the entire mountain range to a greater radiation risk. No one knows how bad it was or what it might mean for those exposed to the radiation but I had found a mate upon whom I could depend if my survival were in jeopardy.

Survival in jeopardy. I had always felt that my survival was tenuous, that I was stuck at the bottom of Maslow's hierarchy of human development, the place where having one's physiological needs met is imperative in order to survive. *Did I have the right to survive? How could I prove that I did have that right?*

To prove my right to survive I set myself two culturally incompatible goals. I would have children and a successful academic career: survival of my progeny, kids *and* ideas. *Having it all,* as it came to be called, was unheard of for girls growing up when I did. So, who would want to marry a PhD woman who wanted a demanding career and children? I had other criteria, too. My husband had to be tall, neither a Christian nor an atheist, and skilled in the Socratic method of arguing that I had embraced in college. Liking classical music gave my imagined suitor extra credit. My time for finding a mate was running out.

I was 22. Herb was tall, handsome, and an agnostic enamored of the late Beethoven Quartets, proficient in Roman, Greek and Nordic mythologies, and a graduate of Reed College where Socrates was the Mascot. And, he was the only man I had dated who acceded to my career and family plans. This was 1959.

A visit with Uncle Mike, Katie's father…

The Cuban Missile Crisis (War!) is averted, Benjamin's enrolled in nursery school, and I have a secure professorship. I allow myself to recognize that my marriage is on shaky grounds.

Herb is consuming six bottles of home-brew a night, home-made mead on weekends, implying that I am having an affair with a colleague, while he spends an extraordinary amount of time trying to prove Fermat's last theorem. Some of the characteristics that had attracted me to Herb—his crassness, his inability to small talk, his irreverence toward upper-middle-class values—were wearing on me, no longer attractive. I had heard that the same characteristics that attracted you to a marriage brought you to a divorce. That, of course, was not going to happen because I don't have the will to violate my father's ethical principles. He defends murderers and thieves but never takes a divorce case because he insists that "divorce is immoral."

My relationships with my parents and siblings are on shaky grounds, too. They don't like Herb. My brother chose not to invite me or "the jerk," as he called Herb, to his lavish Long Island wedding. My brother-in-law imitates Herb's quirky giggle—"heh…heh…heh." My father writes me that he is "disappointed" in my choice of marital partner. Jessica comments that Herb never looks her in the eyes, and that he lacks "social graces." Herb isn't happy in my upper-middle class world, either. He seems to take pleasure in taking off his sandals at the dinner table to pare his toe-nails with his pocket knife.

Aunt Ceil writes to remind me that I am living not far from my Uncle Mike. She sends him my address. Soon, I receive a long typed letter from Uncle Mike: "I would be honored if Herb, Benjamin and my Glorious Niece could find the time to visit in Los Angeles…Come on a Saturday night…Spend the night…Maybe go to the theater…Get a baby-sitter for my Great-Nephew…We're family…All family has to do is rub noses and purr…"

I haven't seen Uncle Mike since I was seven when he had come to Chicago with Katie for Passover. But his letterhead intrigues me: FOREMAN'S MAIL ORDER BOOKS: BY MAIL ORDER ONLY.

***

"Welcome! Welcome! Welcome!" Uncle Mike stands in the driveway greeting us with such gusto that he can probably be heard all over Hollywood. His property is large, mostly undeveloped, and abuts the iconic H-O-L-L-Y-W-O-O-D letters. He hugs me, kisses both of my cheeks, holds my hand to his heart. He looks like Katie and my Aunt Ceil, same blue eyes, porcelain skin. "Let me look at you," he says. "Yes! You look like my dear sister, Rose, and my best friend, Tyrrell."

I wonder how he can think a sister "dear" and a friend "best" if he's not been in contact with them for two decades but I shrug off my wondering.

"Come in…Come in," Uncle Mike says, ushering us into the kitchen of his California bungalow. "And this must be the man who won your beautiful heart."

"…yes, Herb…"

"…and this Nordic-Child-God must be Benjamin…"

"…yes."

"And I am your Great-Uncle...How do you do, Benjamin?"

"Hi!" Benjamin says. "Hot!"

"How delicious that you are named after my father—your grandfather, Baruch," Uncle Mike says to Benjamin, giving him a hair-tussle.

"Well, no...he's not," I say.

"I wanted to name him *Thor*," Herb says, accepting Uncle Mike's handshake.

"Can I give Benjamin a pretzel?" Uncle Mike asks.

"He loves them," I say.

"Come, sit down." Uncle Mike points to the kitchen chairs around the table set with deli-food. "Just like Ma used to make."

Benjamin settles with a giant pretzel in front of a television set, turned off. He has never been this near a television on or off. We don't believe in television. Benjamin reaches for the knobs.

"Not to worry," Uncle Mike says. "The set is broken."

Herb takes a fistful of pastrami. Uncle Mike makes a cole-slaw and corned beef sandwich on rye. I follow suit.

"Take more," Uncle Mike says to Herb, pointing to the pastrami.

Herb heaps more pastrami on his plate. Uncle Mike pats him on the shoulder.

"We already love each other, so let's get to know each other," says Uncle Mike.

He's right. I love this man, already.

"Aunt Gladys is sorry she can't be here." Uncle Mike pets my shoulder the way I would pet a kitten, gently, rhythmically, and perhaps the way he petted Gladys, and maybe Katie, too. "But the depression part of Gladys's manic-depression has landed her back in the hospital. Probably for six months this time."

"My mother's nutty, too," Herb says through his chomping.

"Your Mother must have told you about Gladys's illness," Uncle Mike says. He adjusts his rimless glasses.

I shake my head. "Mother never gossips," I say. "Or tells secrets." I quickly cover my implicit rudeness, "Not that being manic-depressive should be a secret." I don't say that when Katie and I were pen pals, she demanded I keep secret what she wrote to me about her "crazy mother," so, of course, now, I have to feign surprise, keep her secret.

"Do you know Katie's birth-story?" Uncle Mike asks.

I shake my head "no." Herb slathers cole-slaw on a sandwich. Benjamin is transfixed by the television's knobs.

"Well, you do know that I am a Communist, don't you? Uncle Mike asks.

I nod my head yes. Herb is holding his sandwich in his left hand, writing formulae on his yellow-lined note pad with his right one.

Uncle Mike's face gleams as he prepares to tell us the story. "Back in 1935 everyone in my Communist cell were married but we believed in free love. We went on a cruise together, and that's where Gladys and I got together. We divorced our respective spouses and married each other. We named our beloved daughter, Katie, after my ex-wife, after she committed suicide, of course…which was her right, of course…I know your birth story, Laurel…"

"I don't," I interject but Uncle Mike's thoughts have moved on.

"So my beautiful niece tell me about your work and studies."

"My field is the sociology of knowledge," I say. I wait. Uncle Mike looks interested. I continue, "I am interested in how people come to know what they claim to know." I wait. Then, go for it, deploy my academic jargon. "I am an epistemologist, a sociologist who researches how people rationalize their claims to knowledge. My field is called *the sociology of knowledge.*"

My father has never asked me what I study. He has decided that sociology was either "social work" or "socialism" and that was that. No family member has ever asked me about my academic interests. I feel tentative, at first, telling Uncle Mike, and then almost joyous. I had been raised with so many conflicting and incomplete stories, and had been challenged so often about my sense of the truth that I carry scarred childhood baggage with me into my profession. The sociology of knowledge was not my "work," it was my *passion.*

"So, you've studied Karl Marx," Uncle Mike says. He excitedly points to a wall of books.

"Yes," I say, "I have studied Marx." But cautiously speaking now lest I create a rift between us, I say, "I am not taken with him or Marxism."

Uncle Mike weaves slightly in his chair and raises his hands, palm up. "Why?"

I tighten my lips. "Well, for starters, Marx believed that *science* was not subject to epistemological inquiry, and that his *theory* was *science*, and therefore indisputably true."

Uncle Mike counters. "But Marxism matters because of its *moral* position—everyone is taken care of when each works according to his ability and each receives according to his need."

"But, Uncle Mike," I say, drawing upon my minor in political sociology, "where Marxism has been tried, such as in Russia, there is actually more financial inequality than there is in the United States."

"But that's because Russia is only in its socialist stage. The state can't wither away yet because the proletarian state isn't strong enough," Uncle Mike says. He could be reading from the *Communist Manifesto*. It's probably that book I see on a pedestal.

I shake my head. "Are you talking Stalinism now? Ends justifying the means?"

Herb is sitting cross-legged on the floor, his note pad between his knees, an extra sharpened pencil behind his right ear. Benjamin is still engrossed with the television set. I feel good about both Herb and Benjamin looking so comfortable, at ease.

"Okay, Beautiful Niece, I'll retreat," Uncle Mike says. "You deserve your PhD, even if you aren't *yet* a Marxist."

My eyes are tearing up. "Thanks," I say, but that simple word hardly expresses the gratitude I am feeling. Uncle Mike is the first person in my family to engage me intellectually, and the first one to acknowledge that I have an advanced degree. I compare myself to Barrie. Barrie's business doctorate is routinely toted by my father but he never mentions my PhD. "Barrie," he tells others, "is a professor. Laurel is a teacher." Is my having a PhD, especially in that impertinent field of sociology, an embarrassment to him, something outside the approved realm for the genteel woman he wants me to be? I silently laugh. Here I am doing family-epistemology.

"Come and see the rest of my books," Uncle Mike says. "There in the warehouse." He waves behind him. "Just a couple of steps away."

"Benjamin will keep an eye on me here," Herb says, his eyes focused on the formula he is writing.

***

"Carver," Uncle Mike greets a dark-skinned man with a jagged-edged knife-scar down his cheek. He's standing in the warehouse's open door. "Meet my beautiful niece, Laurel."

"G'day, Ma'am," Carver says. He's wearing pocketless coveralls.

"Carver's my foreman," Uncle Mike says, chuckling.

We are just inside the warehouse. Rows upon rows of shelves from floor to ceiling are holding books, spines straight. I have never seen so many books for sale in one place. I can't see any titles. Uncle Mike does not move any further into the warehouse but I can see several dark skinned men in the back shelving and unshelving books. They're wearing coveralls, too. Uncle Mike waves at them.

"Keep up the good work, Carver," Uncle Mike says, as he escorts me out of the warehouse. The H-O-L-L-Y-W-O-O-D sign is in my sight. "Carver's an ex-convict," Uncle Mike says. "All my workers are Black parolees."

"That's nice," I say. I know from my criminology classes that finding work is almost impossible for ex-convicts. My father, the criminal attorney, praised converting Black prisoners to Islam because it reduced recidivism. Could Uncle Mike be winning his workers over to communism?

What would it have been like for Katie to have this warehouse set-up in her backyard? Would she have been frightened by the men? Or enticed?

***

"So where is that Divine great-nephew and Nordic Father-God?" Uncle Mike asks when we re-enter the house.

"Call me Sterculus," Herb calls from the bathroom. "I'm changing Benjamin's diaper."

Herb carries Benjamin back into the living room and settles him by the television.

"My Great-Nephew is so smart," Uncle Mike says. "I love watching him."

"He is intellectually gifted," I say. "Walked and talked at nine-months."

I am moved by how warmly Uncle Mike talks about Benjamin. I decide to take a risk, to tell Uncle Mike something I have kept secret. "He's very smart," I repeat. I breathe deeply and continue, "but he is neurologically challenged."

I look at Herb.

"He has petit-mal seizures," Herb says helping me overcome my reticence.

"From an undiagnosed cause," I say.

"Idiopathic," Herb confirms.

"Not often," I say.

"Happening even less, now," Herb explains.

I have not told my parents or my siblings. If I did, they would blame Herb, shame me, and treat Benjamin as flawed. At least those are my fears.

"That means this Nordic Child-God is attuned to many different ways of the world," Uncle Mike says. "He is more than smart. You'll see. He's a genius."

"Yep," says Herb.

"But I worry," I say.

"He's already a genius," Uncle Mike says. "Look he's fixed the television."

There is no sound on the screen but a lot of fury.

"For a reward, Mister Fixer-Upper," Uncle Mike says. "I'll let you take your father outside to search for our tortoise. He's very old and very big and you can ride on his back."

"Whoopee! Go Da-Dee!"

"Sounds good," Herb says, as he lifts Benjamin to his shoulders and carries him out. "Odin," Herb calls-out. "Come, Odin!"

"Herb is a marvel, a polymath!" Uncle Mike says. "Maybe he has a twin brother? For Katie."

"No such luck," I say.

"I want to show you Katie's room," Uncle Mike says.

"Um—okay."

"See the sleeping porch?" he says as we move out of the living room.

I look at the porch.

"See that couch?"

I see a stained green couch.

"Our Beloved Katie has sex-trysts on that couch." Uncle Mike is glowing. "We could hear her."

"Had," I say.

"Like all teens, she experimented with uppers and downers."

"I missed those experiments," I say.

Uncle Mike persists. "Sometimes, I thought she and her mother would kill each other."

"With knives?" I ask.

"I had to make a choice, of course," Uncle Mike says. "I had to choose my wife, Gladys. Our ties to our darling Katie would be completely severed if not for the allowance I send her...for her dance career...Well, come now—let us enter the Beloved's room. We've left it just as it was when she moved to New York."

I straighten a corner of the rumpled top-sheet on her single bed.

"She never made her bed," the proud father says. He re-rumples the corner.

I look at the jars of grease-paint on her dresser.

"Here, take a whiff," Uncle Mike says. He removes the cap on one of the jars and places it under my nose. Uncle Mike takes a long inhale, replaces the cap and puts the jar back into its place on the dresser.

I am growing numb.

"These are dance companies that were fortunate to feature Katie," Uncle Mike says pointing to posters of companies whose names I don't recognize. "This Nutcracker King was a gift from one of her many admirers."

The king is over two feet tall. I reach to pull the lever that will open his mouth but restrain myself.

"These are her dance costumes," Uncle Mike says waving his hand at the open closet full of leotards, gowns and tutus. "Who knows when she will want them back?"

I remain silent.

"Beloved Katie was a gifted dancer from the moment she was born. She danced and danced and danced…She was a free spirit, a nymph…When she was a teen-ager, I would nestle in my recliner and await her nude entrance."

I stop listening. I am looking at a life-size black and white photograph of Katie, nude. Across her naked abdomen, she has written her name in bold black letters: LAURA FOREMAN.

1980…New York City…

Katie and I stay in a state of knowing-about-the-other through our Aunt Ceil to whom I write banal bi-monthly letters. When I write that I am getting remarried and would be honeymooning in New York City, she insists that I get in touch with my Cousin Katie.

Katie greets Ernest and me at the door to the loft she shares with her husband, the composer, John Watts. Katie and John give *Choreo-Concerts* at The New School for Social Research. John is too depressed to meet us but Katie is energetic. It passes my mind that Katie might try to seduce my husband, but she doesn't nor does she act seductively toward Ernest's brother when he joins us for dinner. I think, she is done with "free love."

One corner of the Foreman/Watts loft is dominated by a grand piano, the grandest piano I have ever seen outside a concert hall. Across from the piano are long folding tables. On them are Brown monotone posters advertising *Wall Work,* a never existing "sold-out" performance, a *New York Times* glowing review of that "happening," photos of a chocolate-covered Statue of Liberty melting in a gallery window, objects found in the gutters of NYC, and Katie's bricolage art—pointy beer can-tops as tits, pink bras as lips, Brillo pads as pubic hair.

Katie and I size each other up, play-act at being blood relatives. Neither of us brings up my brother, her parents, our childhood correspondence or her invasion into my college space, friends, and love-life. I don't mention my visit to her childhood home, the enshrinement of her bedroom, and my conversations with her father. We are polite, cool, and talkative. She is "making it" in New York

City; I am "making it" in a top-ranked sociology department. I am heartened that both of us are successful.

Ostensibly, our worlds are different but our interests are actually similar. Katie is a dancer who is also a writer; she uses "found objects" to make art. I am a sociologist who is also a poet. I use "found poems," snippets of overheard conversations, public signage and quotes from in-depth interviews. Through art, she is deconstructing societal attitudes toward women, and I am doing the same deconstruction through feminist theory.

As I write about this now, I realize how similar we were in our practices despite the great differences in our childhoods. I've heard that said about twins who are raised apart.

2001…This is a hard part…

May 4, 2001. Chambers street is too congested for the cabbie to get through. He leaves me and my suitcase on Church, a block away from Katie's loft. Cars screech. Sirens blast. I walk past ethnic restaurants and shops, and "teeming masses of people yearning to be free" from the plastic bags of garbage spilling out on the sidewalk, the putrid smells filling their nostrils, and mine. I am in a third-world country. A war zone.

"Katie, I'm here," I say on my cell-phone when I reach the dented door of 39 Chambers. Katie's brain cancer has invaded her ears. She told me to phone because she cannot hear the door-bell.

"I'll buzz you in," she says.

I hear the buzz and easily push open the unsecured door. I smell urine.

"I'm on the second floor," Katie yells.

She lives in a five story walk-up above an Indian restaurant. She moved there after her husband's suicide two decades ago. The blackish mailboxes are filthy and small, illegible names scrawl over previous illegible names. Legible obscenities cover the plaster-pealing walls. Scraps of lettuce, Naan crusts, cigarette butts and tumbledown stacks of undelivered flyers crowd the unpainted rickety stairs, treads pulled away from the risers. No banisters. I struggle with my weekender. What must this nightmare be like for Katie?

"Welcome," Katie says. She is standing barefoot by her open door in an open Japanese kimono. Her skin is sallow, her breasts sag, her pubic hair gone. She's half the size she was when I last saw her twenty years ago. I am not sure if I will hurt her if I touch her.

"Come in," she says. I set down my suitcase. She leans into my body, her arms reach for my shoulders, her head rests on my chest, under my chin, on my heart. I hug her. We stay like this, intimate for a minute—or an eternity. "I'm so glad you've come," she says.

Katie steers me into a large, overheated room where a floor lamp sits beside a camping cot outfitted with a pillow and comforter. There is barely enough room to walk around the cot. Tables and shelves hold bins of doll parts, pieces of cloth, broken dishes, marbles, beads, plastic fruit, and lipstick tubes.

Near the window, shade drawn, at least two dozen cardboard boxes teeter atop one another. A ficus plant languishes on a file cabinet. Carpentry tools on pegboard cover one wall, enlarged photos of what look like cancer cells cover another. Books, file-cabinets and out-of-the ordinary bird-houses encircle the room.

I set my suitcase on the cot. It sags. Katie points to a pile of papers on a small table and says, "Here's all the news about my cancer."

I see a bed piled high with quilts and comforters, bottles of prescription drugs, stuffed animals, clothes, and books. The table beside the bed holds a phone, a dozen pair of reading glasses, chocolate wrappers, jelly beans, tumblers, yet more prescription bottles. "My space," she says. "Bathroom back." She points behind her and I see a galley kitchen where a man is eating.

"I'm Robert, Laura's partner," the man says, coming out of the kitchen. "Laura has been eagerly awaiting your arrival."

Robert is a handsome enough man, tall and husky, balding, with a scraggly graying beard. He has a Boston accent. I didn't know that Laura had a partner.

"I don't stay here or anything," Robert says. "I just help out...I hope you like how I set up your cot...and, if you want some air, it is totally safe to leave the window by the fire-escape open at night."

I raise my eyebrows.

"Well, safe enough," Robert says. "Ha-Ha!"

"Help me get dressed, Laurel," Katie points to a crimson colored dress on the bed. She drops her kimono to the floor, lifts her arms and I put the dress on over her naked body. "Those shoes," she says, pointing to a pair of black slippers.

"I'll do it...I know how to adjust her big-toes," Robert says. "How's that, Sweetie?"

"I need to go to the oculist," Katie says. "I need reading glasses."

"I'll come with you, Sweetie," Robert says.

"No!" Katie says. "I want to be alone with my sister, Laurel."

"You mean cousin," Robert says.

"No. Laurel's my sister. Sister."

Robert carries Katie and her walker down the stairs. He snags a taxi that takes us to Cohen's Optical. It is busy. Mr. Cohen recognizes Katie.

"How can I help you, Miss Foreman," he asks.

"Why do you keep selling me glasses that I can't read with?"

"I am so sorry you are having trouble," he says.

I tap my head. He nods. He understands that the brain cancer has affected her optical nerve. "Try some glasses on...help yourself... here's a reading test-card."

"I've taken care of her for over twenty years," Mr. Cohen whispers to me. "I am so sorry."

Katie tries on a pair, rejects it, tosses it on the counter. She tries another and another and another, rejecting, tossing. "Your glasses are shit!" Katie yells.

A customer pulls her purse closer to her hip. Another takes her son's hand and leads him out of the store.

"Maybe they'll work better at your loft," I say. "That's happened for me...different light...less commotion..."

"Yes," says Mr. Cohen. "Take these." He hands Katie a handful of reading glasses. She puts them in her purse. "No charge," he says. "Thank you," he mouths to me.

"We pulled that one off, didn't we, Laurel!" Katie is ecstatic.

I manage to hail a taxi to take us to the Japonika Restaurant, Katie's favorite.

"Greeting, Miss Laura," the hostess says, bowing slightly. "So good see you."

"Niko, meet my sister, Laurel," Katie says. "She's come from Ohio."

Niko bows and waves. "O-hi-o," she says. "Hello."

"We'll have whatever Aki recommends today," Katie says. While we wait for the sushi, Katie tells me that she has come to this restaurant for over twenty years. Niko and Aki and their children are almost like family. Three Japanese children come to our booth and give little bows to Katie. She bows back, pats a girl's hair. The girl bows to me and I pat her head, too. Katie says, "Himari thinks you're my sister."

Between bites of sushi, Katie says, "Diana Ross overcame many obstacles being Black and gay...cutting edge...like old-time jazz...I should buy back my old tenor...Diana had five kids with three different fathers...I don't have much time...I could have had a family...I could have adopted an older child...I would have been a good mother...I regret that I had that abortion...Kids would bother me...Verbal corporeal punishment...Diana is the diva of all divas... How much time do I have?...Rembrandt lived in a Jewish ghetto... Jewish models...Maybe married a Jew...If you don't want any more pogroms, be a commie...I'm on a sabbatical from my psychiatrist... I'm going to pieces without falling apart..."

"I made that," Katie says, pointing to a bird-house in the park. "Tongue depressors, mostly. Fake hundred dollar bills. That's what's happening here in SoHo." She points to the condo developments framing the park. "Everything turns into money. Even a sweet innocent birdhouse."

"I love birdhouses," I say.

"I've made seventeen of them...I think...maybe fourteen...or..."

"I love birds, I think of birds as angels," I say wanting to tell her that the spring when I was in such pain with sciatica that the only thing that got me out of bed was coming downstairs to my sun porch to see the birds. But I don't.

"I love the birds, too," she says. "They're here, but they can always take off."

Robert meets our cab and helps Katie back to her loft. "This card was left under the door, Sweetie," he says, handing her an envelope. "I'll see you tomorrow, Laurel…If you need anything, here's my number."

"Open the envelope, Laurel," she says. "Who is it from?"

"Your neighbors."

"Read it."

"Your neighbors are sorry you are ill, appreciate the courage you have shown, and are sending their love and affection."

"So?"

"They are also asking that you not turn on your gas stove or run the water."

"Why have they turned on me? I am baffled. I am still *Laura*." Katie is fuming. She throws a pill bottle toward the ceiling.

"To me, you will always be Cousin Katie," I say. "K-A-T-I-E… I bet I am on the only one who calls you Katie!"

Katie slyly smiles and nods, confirming my claim to our special relationship without voicing it. "Laurel, you are a good writer," she says. "Write for me." She dictates a letter I type into my laptop:

> Why this sudden rage towards me? I have discussed this with my sister, Laurel. My friend Alma has made a strange alliance with Robert and together they are trying to take over decisions about my life. A few days ago, Alma tried to turn on the stove and heard clicks. She thought that was a sign of danger and made Robert turn off the gas. My fears about her have been substantiated. She cannot be trusted. I hope you will continue to support me in the gracious manner you have so far.

Your neighbor of twenty-one years,

Laura Foreman

"Do you want to respond to the 'turn off the gas and don't run water' requests?" I ask.

"Tell them *okay*."

I don't say, how then will we bathe? Or drink?

"Want some Wild Turkey?" Katie asks.

"I'll pass," I say.

I leave Katie chugging Wild Turkey, put my comforter and pillow on the floor, keep the fire-escape window closed and locked, and pop two Restorils.

***

"I'll turn the water on for you," Robert says. "If you want to take a shower." He hands me a washcloth and towel. He arrives this morning with coffee, bagels, lox and cream cheese. "Katie's favorite."

"Mine, too," I say.

"Eat, Sweetie," I hear Robert coaxing Katie.

"You bastard!" she screams. "You stole my oxy…"

"Here's some, Sweetie," Robert says. "I saved it for you."

Robert dresses Katie in the same crimson dress she wore yesterday. He carries her and her walker down the stairs and hails us a cab. Katie wants me to see her dance studio at The New School. We come to a building, smaller than my Chicago high school, nestled between other buildings of similar lack-luster. I am surprised at how small The New School is compared to the universities in my life.

"So glad you're here," Debbie says, helping Katie out of the cab. Debbie, who looks to be in her forties, is a member of Katie's dance company.

"And you must be Laurel," Debbie says. "Laura's so happy you are here."

Debbie opens the front door, and then another that opens onto a performance stage. Katie beams.

"This is my space," Katie says. "Tell her, Debbie."

"We do share it with the drama groups," Debbie says, "but, yes, it is Laura's space."

"Open the curtain!" Katie orders. "Show my sister the seats."

"Sister?" Debbie says. She looks me over. "Yes, I can see the family resemblance."

"Actually, we're twins," Katie says. "Separated at birth."

I shake my head, "No," point to Katie's head and say, "Don't we wish!"

"I want to have twins," Debbie says.

"You'll have to snort them," Katie says, laughing.

"Laura is going to help me find sperm donors," Debbie says. "Or I am going to adopt or maybe have a surrogate. I have the money. Or will. When my grandmother dies I will inherit her loft and I could sell it…but I don't know how good a mother I would be…I could adopt from China or Ecuador but I want my twins to look like me…"

Katie isn't listening. I am sure she has heard Debbie's litany of uncertainty before.

"That would be nice," I say to Debbie to be polite, although I am not sure what part of her speech I am responding to.

Katie is dancing with her walker, humming, scratching her pubis. She falls.

***

When we get back to her loft, Katie takes some meds, washes them down with Wild Turkey and crawls into bed. I take off her shoes and watch her fall asleep—or pass-out? I have never been with someone sick like Katie. I want to understand, and be understanding, not judgmental. I think she wants me to understand, perhaps even needs me to, and that's why she showed me how to find her "cancer news." I read.

Katie has had lung cancer for five years and has been treated with chemotherapy, radiation and alternative therapies, including an "immune-enhancing tonic" that cost $5,000 a month. In September, 2000, a new tumor in her brain affected movement and cognitive function. Later that month, an MRI showed more brain cancer— leptomeningeal cancer in the tissues surrounding the brain and spinal cord. It is a rare and aggressive cancer that hits nerve, hearing, seeing, face muscles, cognition and ability to balance. The longest life span of a person diagnosed with this kind of cancer is 9 months.

I can't imagine how awful this must be for Katie—not the imminent death but the losses during the dying. A visual artist who can't see. A conceptual artist who can't think straight. A choreographer who can't hear music. A dancer who can't balance.

I rifle through the cancer-news stack and pull out an email Katie's friend, Julie, had sent to their extended community of artists and dancers. The email asked that the community join in a "visualization" on May 1, 11:00–1:00, when Katie will have a follow-up MRI. The request includes two pages of directions. The community visualization failed.

I understand now why I am here. I am her last hope.

Robert brings us Chinese for dinner.

"Eat, Sweetie," he says. "Chicken cashew in brown sauce. Your fave."

"Mine, too," I say.

"Get it away from me!" Katie shouts. "Where's my oxy?"

Robert fumbles in his pocket and takes out a plastic bottle. "Here, Sweetie. I was protecting it *from* you."

Katie shakes the bottle. "You Goddamn shitface bastard. You took some." She puts a capsule in her mouth.

"I had just one…or two…," Robert says. "But I'll call Doctor Smith to re-fill your script."

"Pack my papers and books. Go!"

"Papers?" I ask.

"Laura's and John Watts' papers are going to the New York Public Library Archives," Robert says.

"Laurel's a writer," Katie says. "Her books should be archived with mine…She's my sister…send me your books, Laurel. Robert tell her!"

"Send Laura your books," Robert says.

"Robert means well," Katie says, then whispers, "I have a secret."

"What?"

"I can't walk."

***

An oncological social-worker comes. She says, "Yesterday's history, today's a gift, tomorrow's a mystery." Katie does not seem comforted by those words. I think she's heard it all before.

She tells the social worker, "I was in the detox hospital, once. I don't think I had a moral weakness. Alcohol…cocaine…medicine believes alcoholism is a progressive disease and that I could die of *that*...and the only way is not to drink at all...or smoke smack...I sure fooled those fuckers!"

For the next few days, we do not leave the apartment. Katie's radio blares at night. She's afraid to sleep. Many friends visit, most bring healthy food that Katie rejects, or jelly beans or wine, that she welcomes. Some pass her pills, maybe just vitamins. I don't know. I don't ask.

She tells me what I should do before I go back to my home in Ohio.

"Don't throw away any of my researches...files...boxes."

"Give my bed away! Throw it in the dumpster!"

"Take my money and buy back Robert's Baritone."

"Don't wear any of my cheap clothes. Tuck in the shirts."

"Take a glass shard."

"Be happy."

"Take-out any sexually explicit materials in my notebooks."

"Destroy the sex tapes."

"Put a Post-it on anything you want. Robert will send it to you."

"Destroy photos in red copper box that my mother has. Make sure she knows they were Dad...Not me."

"Come back soon, Sister," Katie says. "Be happy."

This next part will be easier to write. Maybe.

It is so good to be back in my own home—tidy, quiet, clean, safe, cool, clutter-free, alcohol free, pantry full, freezer full, refrigerator full, water on, gas on—and to look upon the green expansive backyard, irises, lilies, American Elm, and the sundial inscribed with the saying, "Grow Old With me...The Best is Yet to Be."

I unpack my suitcase. I inscribe copies of my authored books to Katie. Ernest takes them to the UPS. I feel good being busy. I decide to Fax Katie every day giving her news about my life as if my life might matter to her if I can show a direct link between hers and mine.

"Ernest and I went to Inniswood, a public garden with
a raised wooden walkway. I love those. Do you?"

"I can see you making lists in your head and telling me secrets. I am making lists and thinking of secrets I might tell you."

"I took a long walk through a second growth forest. It reminds me of us. We were children in our first growth."

"Do you recall me saying I was having trouble finding a writing topic? Well, I found my topic. It is US! Cousins!"

Robert phones. "Laura says call the book, *Twin Sisters*."

"I would like some pictures of Katie," I say.

"Her mother has destroyed them all," Robert says. "It broke Laura's heart."

"It's breaking mine, too."

"What's this?" Ernest asks, unpacking a large box. In it are Katie's things that I had put a Post-It on. Robert has sent them.

Ernest pulls out the wire Ferris wheel from the box.

"Is this a Calder?" he asks.

"Yes," I say. "Katie ran in his circle."

Ernest laughs at my attempt at a visual pun.

"What's this?" He takes out a birdhouse.

"That one's called, *Raisin' the Roof*," I say, pointing to raisins shellacked on the house.

He pulls out another birdhouse.

"That one's *Tenement*," I say. Five stark birdhouses are stacked one on top of the other. "It's Katie's statement about the architectural sameness of public housing."

"I'll paint it," Ernest says. "The houses will look different but unified and look like ours. Red roofs on them all." To each house he adds a bird he has fashioned from copper. Two black crows arrive beneath the birdhouse. They are having a great time hopping and eating and flying, together and alone.

But looking at the birds and writing love-notes to my age-mate Cousin Katie does not dispel my moodiness, dysphoria, dis-ease. She is dying at the same age from the same disease as my mother had. It is not about death as much as it is about life. How do I want to live my life? *Can the best be yet to come?* My closest friend, Betty, is acting as if she is terminally ill when she is not. She has shut down her life. She is living to die. But, Katie never shuts down. She's always choosing life. Am I using my cousin's dying to examine—perhaps change—my own life? *Why does it always have to be about me?* I am choked with sadness.

Debbie calls. "Laura said I should tell you how much she loves you. She also wanted me to tell you that your being here were the best weeks of her life."

Robert phones, "Laura is being taken to Cabrini."

"Cabrini?"

"Hospice."

I am in a dark place...dark thoughts...nightmares...

Staying in bed...not caring where anything goes after I die.

"Your room key will get you into our gated park," the desk clerk at Cabrini's hotel tells me. The hotel is simple and clean. I feel safe. I am glad that I have come. Everything about this neighborhood feels so different from Katie's neighborhood. I could be somewhere else. And I am. And so is she.

"She's in 1014," the Cabrini volunteer tells me. I read the sign on the wall-hung fountain: "Don't Drink the Water. It has Chemicals." *Doesn't everything? Doesn't chemo?* I am taking my time, as if doing so will give Katie more time in this world.

Her double patient room is divided by an opaque white curtain. Katie is on her back, her head way back on a pillow on a raised hospital bed near the window. "PT Prefers LAURA" says the placard above her bed. A cold wrap is on her forehead, left arm akimbo, right wrist cocked, fingers fisted. Hospital gown half off. Mouth open. Left eye locked closed. Black metal rimmed glasses on her cheek bones. I stop myself from wailing. She takes my hand.

"Laurel...sister...you've come," Katie whispers.

"She's confused," says Nurse Mary Margaret. "But she's still wonderfully optimistic."

"Hi, *Sister* Katie," I say.

"Need to strengthen my legs," Katie says. "I want to see the scan."

"She's still razor sharp," says Nurse Mary Margaret. "But, no, she can't stand. She's lost soft tissue."

"No standing for you, today," I say.

"She is not going to lose her mind," the nurse says to me in a voice loud enough for Katie to hear.

"Here," I say, putting two birds I created from found objects on her table. "Here we are."

"Don't give the archives what John Watts took," Katie whispers to me. "The sexually exploitive S and M photos…not exclusively heterosexual…Swingers magazine…"

"I won't," I say, although I know I am lying. The archives have already left her apartment.

"My Bank Book?"

"Here," I say, "In the drawer.

"Did I hide it there?"

"It was safe there…we found it."

"Laurel, Laurel, Laurel…I'm dying."

"The Lord is your shepherd, he shall preserve your going forward and your coming in…," a man's voice comes from the neighboring bed, 1013. "You're going home today."

"He's not talking about you," I say. "It's your roommate." *Why do they put someone who is dying in a double room?*

"He's not talking about *home*," Katie says. "He means she's dying today."

A yellow legal pad is on her table. Visitors have written notes. Most ask is she wants to eat something. Others talk about work. One says, "You're going to be okay." *I don't think so.*

"John will put me out of this research, he'll put me out of this museum," Katie says. *John died twenty years ago.* "They'll take pink feathers out of the Eskimo's ass, so take me out of here…They take my pens away, my wrists away, take him away please."

"The clouds are really beautiful today," I say. "Take a look." I raise Katie's bed higher. "See, they are a little world with their own little cities and farms."

"At Great Gull Island I sometimes take pictures of amazing clouds," Katie says.

"The terns are returning!" I laugh at my little pun. "They need a birdhouse."

"I had the spring band concert tonight," Katie says. "It went well. I'm so tired."

"I'll go to the little park, watch the clouds, and let you sleep."

"Laurel, you are beautiful," Katie says. "I am getting my duffel bag so I can spend the night…with you…at the park…"

The park is a green refuge from the antiseptic hospice. Children giggle here, not moan. Trees here not Cabrini nuns. One plaque honors the garden's benefactor. No crucifixes. I am buoyed thinking about how Katie has lived her life—feisty, grateful for beauty, and jelly beans.

Robert is at Katie's side when I return. "Roll on your back, Sweetie," he says. "Here comes the nurse with some real sweet Lax."

"Last night," Katie says, "I let students stay in the lab 'til after eleven p.m. to study. They're having their midterms tomorrow."

"That was kind of you," I say.

"You're a very good twin sister."

"Thank you. You are a very good twin sister, too."

I am a bit obsessed. I want to record everything, everything about Katie's dying, as if recording it will prevent it or least memorialize it. But I edit and condense.

The phone rings steadily. Aides come and go. "Is your back comfy?…Can I put you a little higher?…Is that better or worse…Does it hurt there?…Would you like more ice cream?…You can do it where you are, I will clean up later…Orange juice?…That's what catches the urine…Do you think you need a pill?…We'll get ginger ale in a minute… Would you like some yogurt?…How about some gentle stroking?…Can you swallow a larger pill?…Please swallow the two decaden pills in your mouth so you don't choke or spit them out…Are you wet?"

I am never asked to leave her room. I try to ignore what I see and hear. *Privacy? Dignity? Hers? Mine?*

Laura is asleep when Debbie arrives. "Tell Laura I got her more eyeglasses," she says, leaving a plastic bag on the window sill. "Tell her I'm going to the Cape for the weekend. I'm interviewing a possible sperm donor. Tell her he's a doctor!"

Five more friends come. We talk about Katie in the third person. I say, "Dying is not about people." *What can I possibly mean by that?*

I put lotion on Katie's long legs, just as I did on my mother's two days before she died.

Two nurses quarrel. Here, in her room, as if she is not here. As if I am not here. But I am here in Katie's space with time to write and draw. I draw her hand and she moves it. I draw down to her chest, as if my pen is moving her, helping her breathe. *What am I doing? My cousin as art object?*

Katie reaches for my pen and steno pad and scribbles on it.

"I can't quite read this," I say.

"Iz...my...name."

I decipher *L-I-F.*

Katie does not have a middle-name. Maybe she is writing *Life.*

***

Six-thirty a.m. Laura takes her pills: percoset, lantin, axyclouis, atvian. Needs to take: Paxil, nontriptyline, clonazepan, oxycontin (30 mg), decodron.

"Are you hot?" Doctor Smith asks.

"No."

"Pain?"

"My pain feels like a cat or a rabbit farting."

I squeeze her hands.

"I want to go home," Katie points to a nurse."Look! She has GOD GOD GOD written on her forehead. I am afraid."

"Afraid to stay here?" I ask.

"Yes...They'll make me believe in God."

Those are the last words I hear her speak. She has stopped talking. I tell myself to let her go. I take two sleeping pills and bed down on the couch in Katie's room. At five a.m. I hear the orderlies come in, change her sheets and clothes. They are rough and she cries. I hear a priest conducting last rites. I hope Katie can't hear it. No, I realize, he's conducting a prayer service for volunteers. A woman is moved into the bed next to Katie's, 1013. "Isn't that a bad number?" the new hospice patient asks.

At six p.m. Doctor Smith comes in and takes her pulse. "Not yet," he says. "But soon."

"She's stopped talking," I say.

"That's natural," he says. "She's moving away...pulling away."

"How does she finally die?" I ask. "Does the brain cancer stop her breath? Stop her heart? Her will to live?"

Doctor Smith shrugs, "No one ever dies from cancer." He leaves the room.

Do we ever know how someone dies?

Katie looks at me and a wave of sadness comes over her face.

"I feel sad, too," I say. Katie's long legs are bruised. In her blue diapers and lavender gown, legs bent up, she looks like a child. I can imagine her as the child she was when we were first met. And now, here we are.

Katie sleeps. I write on her note pad that when two people who deeply care about each other are asleep at the same time they can share a dream. In my dream last night I was very still, comfy and quiet deep inside, curled up almost like an embryo. A loving arm reached around my back and cradled my head. Katie, I hope you had this dream, too. So much goes on in our sleep.

And then...

Katie dies June 15, 2001. Six truck-loads empty her loft. Her detritus-collection and art supplies go to schools. Her bed is put in the dumpster. *The New York Times* devotes a column to her life as a choreographer, artist and writer. As she had desired, her death is attributed to cancer. The column names only her mother, Gladys, as a survivor. I am disappointed that I wasn't named, and I think Katie would be outraged at the man she'd call "shitface" who wrote the column.

I phone Katie's mother, Gladys. She is 93, living in Sunset Hall in Los Angeles. "Goddamn shame," she says.

"So so sorry," I say.

"There's a hole in my heart," she says, "But you get up in the morning and you eat breakfast and you get used to it."

"So sorry," I say, again.

"Life can play tricks with you," she says. "Child and parents can be mismatched...Really, really...My daughter worried about the birds. For someone else that would be it. My daughter made houses for them."

"She gave me two of those houses," I say.

"Goddamn shame!"

"Katie," I say, "wanted you to know that the photos in the copper red box were never her idea but her father's."

"I don't know what box. I don't have it...My daughter was elegant...I saw that in that six-year old child...Goddamn shame."

We hang up and I wonder why Gladys doesn't ever refer to her daughter by name—neither as Katie nor Laura while I can only refer to her as *Katie.*

And now...

I have kept Katie out of my ongoing daily life for eighteen years. I surprise my sons and closest friends when I tell them I am writing about Cousin Katie. They didn't know I had a cousin Katie, much less that she had died. I had tried to write about her death and dying five years ago but couldn't get past the parts that lived in my childhood memories. She was the only person I had witnessed going through a long agonizing death. And, she was—still is and always will be—my only age-mate cousin. Her death and dying was and still is traumatic: I am seeing how the contours of her life and mine fit together, like the nested seams of a quilt.

I look at the photos I took of Katie's world. I read my fifty or so pages of field notes. Ernest repaints Katie's Tenement birdhouse in our back yard to match the new colors of our house. I bird watch. I have nightmares, body pains, thoughts of death. I worry that one of my twin dogs will get hurt or lost. I wake up feeling for the both of them in my bed. Pet them. Reassuring myself.

I write. I get insight.

From the time we first met as seven year olds, Katie wanted to dissolve the personal boundaries between us. She wanted my life. She wanted to take my name, wear my clothes, borrow my glasses. She chose to have her body penetrated by the guy who had first penetrated mine. Despite all I was unwilling to cut her out of my life. Then, when I was a young wife and mother I visited her father, my Uncle Mike, in her childhood home. That visit changed how I felt about Katie, and, as I realize now, how I feel about myself.

Uncle Mike was a charmer, a seducer, a man-with-a-plan. Most likely, Uncle Mike's mail-order books were banned ones. Most likely, Uncle Mike hoped to win his "workers" over to communism. If he had a nefarious plan in mind for ensnaring me into his politics, that was not what I felt. I felt he was genuinely interested in me, my husband, and son.

He was the first person that I felt loved and accepted me unconditionally. He treated me like the father I wished I had had—a warm father, interested in my scholarship, welcoming to my husband, and adoring of my son—a father I could talk to about my fears, failures and future without trepidation of being judged, rejected, abandoned.

I didn't have that feeling again with anyone until I was in divorce-therapy and the medical student in his psychiatry rotation looked me in the eyes and said something—I don't remember what— but I felt understood. I experienced the feeling I had had with Uncle Mike. I cried.

It has been extremely difficult for me to look at Uncle Mike's dark-side. He was a predator, a delighted voyeur of his daughter's nude body, an ecstatic listener to her orgasmic cries, a proud sanctifier of her troubled life in La La Land, and the blissful enshriner of her bedroom, forever left as she had left it. Uncle Mike had not only sexualized his relationship with Katie, he had memorialized it, kept it alive. He was a horrible father to his daughter, and I am grateful that he was not my father.

Although I couldn't verbalize any of this until now, I must have somehow known it in my heart. Although I lived near to Uncle Mike's house and went to Los Angeles twice a week to teach for another two years, I never again visited him. Nor did I invite him to my house. I never saw him again.

So, I understand why Katie would want my life. She was a "twin-wanna-be." She wanted a father who was not an incestuous pedophile. She wanted a father like mine, distant. I didn't want her life but I did want a father who made me feel that I was justified in being alive. Maybe I was a "twin-wanna-be" too?

I accept that my "story" of being rejected and abandoned in my own family is not a story, but a reality. I survive.

"Laurel, Laurel, Laurel…I'm dying," said Katie. I could not abandon her. Katie and I were enmeshed. Metaphorically, we were conjoined twins: The only way to separate is for one twin to die. Katie died.

CHAPTER 12

LONE TWIN

From the beginning of my life, my siblings treated me badly. I think that whenever they experienced loss or suffering, they revisited what they thought was the indisputable and inescapable cause of their childhood discontent: my existence.

When I am thirty-three years and recently divorced from Herb, Jessica visits me in Ohio. It is going on midnight and we are sitting, sideways, on my white velvet couch. We're drinking Scotch and eating pretzels.

"I hated you," she says, chugging a large tumbler of Scotch.

I have long felt that she didn't like me. But hate me?

"Mother and Father were always saying how perfect you were." She refills her tumbler to the brim. I take a sip from mine.

My parents had bragged that baby Jessica would be smart and gorgeous, just like them. But homely Jessica didn't walk or talk until eighteen months. They were being punished, Mother said, for their arrogance.

"I was a dud!" Jessica empties the Scotch bottle. "They called me that. A *Dud*! You, they called '*Perfect*. Little Miss Perfect!'"

***

I am forty and visiting my brother, Barrie. He has invited six of his best friends to meet me.

"When Laurel was just in the fourth grade, she won the Chicago Spelling Bee," he says. "While I was the first one down and out in my classroom's bee." Is he bragging about me, or himself?

"I didn't win all of Chicago," I protest. "Just the north side."

"Only because Father wouldn't let you compete in the bad neighborhoods," Barrie says. "To protect *Little Miss Perfect*."

Perfect? Me? "In first grade, I misspelled "girl" as "g-r-i-l.""

© KONINKLIJKE BRILL NV, LEIDEN, 2019 | DOI:10.1163/9789004411364_012

Barrie raises his eyebrows and cocks his head. His friends laugh. I am embarrassed.

"When I was learning dog-paddle," he says, "Little Miss Perfect was winning blue ribbons in the back-stroke."

His friends laugh.

"Although she is almost three years younger, she went to college before I did," Barrie says

"You know that's not true," I say. "We went at the same time because…"

***

This is the story I was told about my birth: On a blistering hot Chicago day in the middle of July my three-year-old brother, Barrie, Aunt Ceil and my mother pregnant with me are at Oak Street Beach. Barrie is chasing sea-gulls. Mother calls for him to come back and not go so far but he doesn't listen or doesn't hear. He keeps running, faster and faster, further and further. Then, Mother screams. She curls up in pain. "My son," she shouts between screams. "My son. Where is my son?"

An ambulance brings her to the Evangelical Deaconess Hospital. All the way there and until the sunrise she prays, "God punish me for leaving my son at the beach. Punish me. Make this baby a girl."

The doctor delays my delivery. I am born. A wet-nurse nurses me.

Father names me, *Laurel*, after his mother and all the other Laurels that have been in our family for generations. A true family name. By naming me Laurel, he tells my mother, he is proving that he wants me. *Was he proving that he wanted a child? A girl? Me?*

***

"When I grow up, I want to have twins," I say to my father. I am six. He is building me a play-kitchen in our basement.

"You can't have twins," Father says. "They skip generations."

"What are generations?" I ask. But he can't hear me over the pounding.

***

I am thirteen, working at Goldblatt's Department Store, starting Senn High School and receiving a $5.00 a week allowance, a large sum back then with which I pay street-car fares, lunches, school supplies, books, savings, toiletries, and clothes with the exception of my winter coat and shoes. Mother considers those "necessities."

"The year you were born," Father tells me, "I had scarlet fever and Barrie was in the hospital——brought back to life after his heart had stopped." Father pauses and says, "I was $20,000 in medical debt by the end of the year…I paid back every red nickel." Why is he telling me this?

***

When I am fifty, a first cousin on my father's side sends me our family-tree, as compiled by my father for my cousin's daughter. The genealogy dates back to the 1700's. There are no Laurels. My father's mother's name is not Laurel, it is *Matilda.*

What else about my birth-story is untrue? What woman in the late 1930's would go swimming at a downtown Chicago beach when she was very pregnant? Why a wet-nurse? Why would a doctor delay delivery?

Some issues have dogged me all my life: Do I have the right to survive? Why do I abhor the idea of living alone while, nevertheless, collecting a shelf of memoirs written by women who do live alone and, although I mercilessly prune my library, I don't pluck-out any of those books? And, why am I so attached to "twinning"——so attached that I have, for example, serially sought a best friend who could be a surrogate twin, developed a deep psychological connection to my age-mate cousin who wanted to be my twin, and awaken much too often from dead-baby nightmares?

***

I am seventy years old, celebrating my birthday with Jessica and Barrie. Jessica is 80. She is at her home in hospice. She has three

111

primary cancers that have metastasized. We are in her living room where she is lying on her green silk couch, pillows holding up her head. She and I are holding hands. I can't tell where her hand stops and mine begins. Her skin feels like my skin.

"Laurel…Laurel," she croons. "You were very sick when you were born."

"I was?"

"You had to have a wet-nurse."

"Hmm."

"You had to stay in the hospital for a long time."

"I did?"

"And we hated you when you came home," Barrie chimes in.

I am surprised to hear him say out loud that which I had felt during most of my childhood. I am angry, too, that he is interrupting these precious moments when Jessica and I are touching each other, familiarly, like sisters can.

"Mother was very sick, too," Jessica continues. I pat her head, smoothing her hair. "Childbirth fever…she had to stay there a long time, too."

"I'm sorry," I say. I sniffle, imagining my sick mother as I sit by my sick sister.

Jessica pats my left hand.

Barrie's face is contorted in anger. He looks at me and says, "You took our good and happy mother away from us! *You* did that, *Baby* Laurel!" He stomps his feet like a child having a tantrum. "Little Miss Perfect!" He bounds out of the room and slams the door behind him.

I am terrified by his outburst and lean my head toward Jessica's seeking solace.

She whispers in my ear "Your twin didn't live."

"*What*? What twin?"

Jessica shakes her head. Zips her lips.

"I'm ordering us Chinese," Barrie says, bringing in a carry-out menu from the kitchen.

When I learn on my sister's deathbed that I am a surviving twin, a secret she had apparently been sworn to keep but at the end of her life found she could not, I am benumbed. The news has come from nowhere. *It is news.* I go into a space familiar to me throughout my life when something I can't or don't want to think about invades my world. I anesthetize myself. Detach from my feelings.

***

I really did not know that I had a twin. I did not have an inkling. There is no material evidence of her existence, or of mine for that matter until I am almost two. It never occurred to me that my fascination for *twinning* was unusual. *Wasn't that something that fascinated every girl? Don't all children think that what they are experiencing is just how things are? Normal?* I never connected my existential fear of living alone, loving the doubling of words and sounds in my writing, and seeking best friends as related to the possibility that I had been a twin.

I live in the anesthetized space regarding my birth for the dozen or so years between my sister's dying and the writing of this book. I keep busy. I write three books and a dozen or so articles. I take on the challenges of caring for grandchildren. I make art quilts, several honoring Jessica and others, like the cover of this book, giving my Twin a material life. I talk to Barrie about politics. I have lunch with friends. And, then…

Out of nowhere, it seems, I wake up one morning wanting a dog. I don't know why. "We'll have to get a dog, then," Ernest says. "So you can find out why." I study dog breeds for about a year, finally deciding that I want a small, smart, beautiful and genetically healthy dog—a Papillon. Ernest and I set up a meeting with a breeder. As fate would have it, she introduces us to *two* Papillon show-dogs, *litter-mates* who have been separated for months. Bashi is a Novice Champion in Canada, but his left front paw turns in slightly and so is not perfect enough to be an American Grand Champion and has been returned to the breeder. Lily has been sold and returned three times. She has had three first names. She weighs two pounds, has failed to thrive, and cannot be shown or bred. I adopt them both.

They run around in circles in my back yard, Bashi chewing Lily's cheek. They sleep on my bed, curled around me. I train them as agility dogs and certified therapy dogs. They work with children who have severe physical and behavioral challenges. I am so proud of and so in love with *my dogs.*

A dream on the anniversary of my sister's death.

In the dream, Bashi and Lily are whispering to each other. They know I am with them, overhearing what they say.

"Which one's life should be saved?" Lily asks.

"We'll know when the time comes," Bashi replies.

CHAPTER 13

FORGIVING MY FAMILY

Our birth wreaked havoc on my family.

Here's what happened to my mother.

Mother's taken in an ambulance to an unfamiliar hospital. She's worried that Barrie is still lost at the beach and hopes he has been found and that her husband is in the waiting room, where the men must wait. She knows what labor feels like, having had two children already, but it is too soon for this child to be born. Someone clamps down her arms and binds her feet to stirrups. Someone puts a mask over her nose and mouth. She breathes in, smells the acrid fruitiness of ether. When she awakens from the sedation, she learns she has birthed two babies—one much weaker than the other.

The weaker baby gets weaker. Mother's desire to hold the baby is denied. The rules prohibit it lest the mother form a bond with the baby. My twin dies without a birth certificate, unnamed. A nurse carries her to the basement, opens the grate and, casts her into the incinerator.

Mother has had the devastating experience of the loss of a newborn, and yet and still she has the surviving baby who needs her. But Mother feels numb, uninterested in the living baby girl, guilty that she had prayed to give birth to a son, and fearful that the living girl, who is sick, will die, too. Mother longs and aches for the baby she cannot hold and feels terrible not to just feel grateful for the one she can hold. "You have one baby," says a nurse. "Some women don't have any."

Mother contracts childbirth fever, which is not a minor inconvenience, a little sweatiness, maybe some chills. No, throughout history it has been the major cause of maternal death. In the 1930's, childbirth fever deaths increases as more women give birth in hospitals, attended to by doctors. The birthing of twins only increases the risk.

© KONINKLIJKE BRILL NV, LEIDEN, 2019 | DOI:10.1163/9789004411364_013

Hospitals were not yet practicing basic hygiene like washing hands, removing bloodied surgical aprons, separating the hospitalized sick from the maternity ward, autopsies from surgeries. Doctors were spreading bacteria, carrying germs from patient to patient. One of the bacterium carried to the maternity wards was the virulent one that caused scarlet fever, rampant in Chicago the year I was born. Antibiotics were years away. Father had scarlet fever. Did Mother? Did I?

My mother suffered through the death of my twin and experienced the stabbing pains of childbirth fever. Her uterus and abdomen are inflamed. Legs throb. Bloody urine. Sepsis. Breasts swollen. Mastitis. Blood poisoning. Dying.

She see sees a wet-nurse holding her living baby across the room.

Here's what happened to my father.

Father worries that Mother will not survive and that if the baby girl does survive, she will be needy and weak. He is overwhelmed with keeping-up his law practice, repaying $20,000 in medical debts, visiting his sick wife, and arranging care for his two young children, one still a toddler. Worse, if his wife should die he will not be allowed to raise his daughters unless he remarries. A single man living with girls is a prosecutable offense in Chicago.

And then there is another issue. When my Catholic raised father married my mother, he promises Mother's mother—Gramma—that the children would be raised Jewish. For Father, the keeping of a promise is the single most important of all possible ethical behaviors: *If he didn't keep his promises, who would he be?*

"Ma," Father says to Gramma. "We need you to raise the children Jewish."

Here's what happened to Jessica and Barrie.

Father buys a "mansion" on Lake Park Avenue on the south side of Chicago. He moves Gramma, Jampa and Aunt Ceil into the servants' wing of the house. Gramma sets up a kosher kitchen and Aunt Ceil prepares to give piano lessons. Father moves Jessica and Barrie from their stable north side neighborhood to a south side one, in transition. Gone are jaunts to Lincoln Park, Belmont Harbor, Lake Michigan. Gone is the friendly policeman on the corner. Street lights. Trees. Grass. Backyard. Gone is Jessica's school. Gone…gone…gone. So much of what my siblings have taken for granted and enjoyed, gone.

Here's what happened to Jessica.

Gramma sends ten-year old Jessica to live with Jewish relatives, the Weisman's, during the school week. The Weisman's have two teen-age sons. The older one, Abe, molests my sister.

On Sunday afternoon, Father spends time with Jessica.

"How do you like your new school?" Father asks.

"Fine," she says.

"Have you made friends there?"

"Yes."

"Do you like your teacher?"

"Yes."

"What is your favorite subject?"

"Gym."

"How do you like the Weismans?

"Fine."

"Nice boys, yes?"

"Y-y-y-es."

Here's what happened to Barrie.

Toddler Barrie's care is entrusted to Gramma, who does not speak English. She follows the Talmudic childrearing practices of Ashkenazi Jews. She watches carefully over Barrie, encourages his learning, insists he wash his hands before eating, takes a hot-bath with oil, and eats only kosher food. Most importantly, she follows the Talmud's medieval guidance in protecting children from the Evil Eye, a malevolent glare that can cause great misfortune. It is as if the Evil Eye sees and governs everything. *Kine Hora!*

Barrie washes his hands in the kitchen sink where earlier a head-less chicken had been bled out. He can still smell the deadness and odd spices. He dries his hands on a red and blue kitchen towel and sits on a raised kitchen chair.

"Essen, Baruch," Gramma says, using Barrie's Hebrew name. On Barrie's plate there is gefilte fish to ward off the Evil Eye.

"No," says Barrie who has never liked smelly food.

"Essen," Gramma repeats putting a chicken leg on his plate. She shakes salt over his left shoulder. "*Kine Hora!*"

"I want milk!" Barrie demands.

"Oy vey!" she says. She shakes her head. *No.*

Aunt Ceil comes in, pats Barrie on the head with one well-manicured hand, protects her chest with the other. She does not like to be touched.

"Bacon?" Barrie asks, hopefully.

"Traife!" Aunt Ceil says, shaking her head in disgust.

"Who is this ugly big boy?" Jampa says, heading off the Evil Eye. Jampa puts a little blue yarmulke on Barrie's head. "There! Baruch. You look like a yeshiva yeled."

Jampa walks Barrie a scant two blocks to Shul. Men in the synagogue are dressed in shawls, hats, and strings hanging out over their pants. "Shalom!" A long-bearded man says, squeezing each of Barrie's cheeks between a thumb and fore-finger. Four other bearded men repeat the greeting and the squeezing. Five times fends off the Evil Eye. The men sing-song in another different strange language. Some men are standing and bowing back and forth. Grown men acting crazy. Fending off the Evil Eye?

Barrie falls asleep. His nightmares feature the Evil Eye.

"Baruch...Baruch," Jampa whispers, waking Barrie up.

"*Baruch atah Adonai...*Barrie rubs his eyes and wonders, *Is the long bearded man calling his new name?* No, because Long Beard is still talking...*v'Shabbot kodsho*"...and he is holding a great big cup. Long Beard pours what looks like cherry juice into little glasses.

"Kiddush," Jampa says, handing Barrie a glass of the wine. "L'Chaim!!"

Here's what happened to Mother and me.

A very long time passes, by Jessica's reckoning, before Father brings Mother and me home from the hospital. Mother is weak, pale, depressed. She has lost weight and hair. She is exhausted from the car trip from the hospital. She is holding me in her arms in a receiving blanket. I have a crocheted hat on my head. Barrie rushes up.

"Not too fast," Mother says. "Not too close. Baby Laurel is weak."

Barrie chews his lip. He puts his hands in his pockets where he can make invisible fists.

"She's pretty," Jessica says, not looking at me.

"She's perfect," Mother says. "Perfect."

"*Kine hora*," Grandma says, frowning.

"Let's hope Baby Layah won't cry when I have piano students," Aunt Ceil says.

" *Layah!! Tova Kindela!*" Jampa carries me into the kosher kitchen and warms a milk bottle. "*Mook, Kindela.*"

Here's what happened to Mother and Father.

Father leads Mother to a first floor room closed off by pocket doors. She collapses on the bed. He pours himself a tumbler of scotch, neat. I am put in a crib in the room where Mother sleeps. I don't know where Father sleeps.

Father has lost the woman he had married. A beautiful, fetching, exotic woman with long black hair and dazzling eyes. His wife is now mired in sorrow, fear, and anxiety. Mother has lost her desire to be desired by this handsome Irishman. How terribly difficult this must have been.

Here's what happened to me.

We live for three years with Gramma, Jampa and Aunt Ceil. Gramma potty trains me. Mother tells Barrie to "wipe my seat." He gags. Pinches my butt cheeks. Squashes his hand over my mouth and nose. I can't breathe.

"She asked for a hammer," Barrie says, after throwing one at my head, just missing.

"She broke the vase!" Jessica says pointing to me. "She slid down the banister and broke it," Barrie says. Mother does not doubt them. I am not yet two.

"Ssh," says Aunt Ceil.

"Mook, Kindela," says Jampa, holding me, giving me my bottle.

Mother sits in the rocker and knits baby-sweaters for other babies.

Father? Somewhere…

I sit in Gramma's kitchen with a towel wrapped around my body and the chair's spindles. I watch her bleed a headless chicken. She wears a kerchief and dark clothes. She never smiles. She smells. She is tall. I can't understand her. I am afraid of her. She calls me *Layah.*

Here's what happened, later.

Jessica moves to Des Moines, marries her high-school sweetheart, and becomes a Head-Start teacher for which Iowa gives her a prestigious award. I wonder if her career trajectory was in part penance for how she treated me when I was a baby and a child.

Jessica loans me $1500 to buy a Morris Minor. She takes care of me and my son, Benjamin, during my post-partum meltdown and my bout of breast fever. She gives me Aunt Ceil's jewelry. When Herb and I divorce, she lends me money to fix-up my house. I never repay her. She never asks.

We meet in Chicago to walk the streets and to be with each other. I help her pass a graduate-school entrance test. We talk on the phone nearly every day. I cross-stitch a wall-hanging, "SISTERS." We know more about each other than anyone else knows about us. We are best friends who love each other.

Barrie and I become friends during our high-school, college and graduate school years—his degree taking him into college administration. During the years of his first marriage we lose that closeness. But when he is contemplating divorce, he comes to see me. He walks around the kitchen table, talking, griping, whining, telling me more than I care to know, asking for more than I am prepared to give.

"Who are you to come here and ask for my support?" I shout at him. I yell at him, he yells at me, and I yell back louder. Then it is over, and we sit down and eat our lunches. Ever since that blow-out, in which neither of us really knew or could express what was really bothering us, we have been good friends.

Barrie becomes a world-class magician, a member of England's exclusive Magic Circle. Magic is a way of foiling the Evil Eye through misdirection giving Barrie a few moments of privacy and peace, his life long struggle to protect himself from the perils of the Evil Eye.

Six years after Jessica's death, Barrie has aplastic anemia. We talk on the phone nearly every day for six months. I help him remember times and places he wants to remember. I put off flying to see him *knowing* that the longer I put it off, the longer he will live. He tells me he is tired of being pricked, wearing diapers, and of people coming to his house talking about events that he won't be alive to take part in. I decide it is time to fly out.

"You were like a little Shirley Temple," he says. "It was like we had our own little family star…so cute…so sweet…"

"I didn't know that," I say. "Tell me more."

He shakes his head and looks alarmed. I think the discomfort my babyhood had created for him had returned. Birth and death, twin-born. He motions for help to get back to bed. He doesn't talk again. He dies two weeks later.

And me?

I know that Father's parents divorced and the youngest four children were raised separately. I open my FATHER file folder, take out the family-tree document and study it. My father's grandmother's name is *Laura,* and his much older sister is named *Laura.* Laura had married a wealthy lawyer and had been entrusted with Father's upbringing.

"Aunt Laura" gave me books, came to my graduations, and gave me a diamond ring.

At her fancy house I saw the trimmings and trappings that my father had luxuriated in and memorialized in his leather photograph album that sits on a shelf in my closet. Aunt Laura raised him. She was his titular *mother.*

"Let's call this baby girl, *Laura,*" I can imagine my father saying, wanting to honor his older sister who had been a *mother* to him and given him a bountiful life.

"We can't do that!" I imagine my Jewish mother near hysteria invoking the belief she grew up with. "If you name a baby after a living person that means you want that person dead."

"Of course, I don't want Laura dead," I imagine my father saying. "But I want to honor her and honor this daughter's victory over death…Let's name her *Laurel.*"

I am Laurel.

FURTHER ENGAGEMENTS

QUESTIONS FOR DISCUSSION

Names:

1. Naming is a central theme in *Lone Twin*. The narrator has three primary names—Laurel, Laurie, and Layah. Her cousin, also, has three primary names—Katie, Laura, Sweetie. Friends and family members' names recur frequently. One unnamed person is named (secretly) by Laurel. The mystery of Laurel's paternal grandmother's name resolves the book. What do you think of the author's use of "naming" as a theme?
2. Why is a *name* so important? What does a *name* reveal? Gender? Age? Ethnicity? Race? Social Class? Birth place?
3. What about your name? Do you use different names in different situations? Have you changed your name? If so, how has that affected you?
4. "Sticks and stone will break your bones/but names will never hurt you," is an eminently false dictum. Being called a "name" can shame, embarrass, and debilitate one. It is not just a poeticism that "naming rhymes with shaming," it is a hard truth that many have lived with. Have you? Or do you come from a family, region, social class or ethnicity that routinely calls people "names"? How do you handle either being called names or being with people who do the calling?
5. We live in a world of gender diversity and transgenderism. How does that reality relate to baby-naming norms? What about pronouns?

Friendship:

1. Friendship is a voluntary relationship. There are no formal rules governing friendship so people are pretty free to develop friendships in different ways. What role has social media played for you in developing, maintaining, and ending friendships? Are

your friendships on social media different than those in "real" life? Have your friendships changed as you have aged? Changed jobs? Changed romantic partners?

2. Who is friends with whom is an indicator of how "open" a society is. In your social world, do friendships cross class, gender, sexuality, ethnicity and racial lines? Are some harder to cross than others?

3. Are there differences in the way females "do" friendship from the way males "do" friendship"?

4. Have you had any "bad" friends?

5. Have any of your friendships been about "twinning"? If so, were you the one seeking the twinning experience or was it your friend? Or both of you? How do you think/feel that a "twinning" experience or lack of one is helping/harming you in shaping your life?

Secrets:

1. Many families keep secrets—sometimes from "outsiders" and sometimes from other family members. Is "secret keeping" passed down through a family? What are some of the consequences of secret-keeping?

2. Sperm donors, bio/technological interventions, and adoption bring new children into families. Modern DNA testing, "23-and Me" saliva kits, and open adoption records bring new information to families, some of which has been purposefully kept secret. Who has the right to know what?
   Are there secret birth stories in your family? How does it feel to keep the secret? Reveal it?

3. "Secrets protect the powerful," is a sociological axiom. Can you provide examples that support or refute the axiom?

4. What do you think children should be taught about lying? Did your family, peer-group and/or community define "lying" in the same way? Do you have to negotiate between different "moral" worlds?

5. What kind of truth is the author telling in *Lone Truth*? Emotional? Relational? Experiential? Personal? Sociological?

Inequality:

1. In 1950, Laurel's high school teacher scrawled across one of her papers, "You would change the world so that you and your kind would get a better deal." Who do you think "your kind" might include today? Race? Gender? Sexual preference? Economic position? Ethnicity? How can the world be changed to improve the life chances of your "kind"? Or, is your "kind" already privileged? Can everyone be the "same kind"?
2. What are some of the ways the people in *Lone Twin* used their privileges to their own advantage? Employed them to help others?
3. Were there any inequalities in *Lone Twin* that surprised you? What about parental role inequalities?
4. During her childhood, Laurel has friends across the economic spectrum—welfare recipients, blue-collar, white-collar, and wealthy. They were also ethnically and religiously diverse. In grade school the girls belong to the same club, but in high school they are separated by religion into Jewish and Gentile sororities. What is it like for you? Are there different "groups" based on social identities?
5. What do you think about inequalities based on "beauty" and/ or "intelligence"? How do you think people should deal with the "beauty" and "anti-aging" discourses in American culture? What about the degrading discourse about less educated people?

Other Themes:

1. Place plays a prominent role in *Lone Twin*. Where we grow up has a profound impact on our lives. Where did you grow up? Did you move to different neighborhoods? States? Countries? How has your geographical mobility (or lack of it) impacted your life?
2. Race, gender, class, ethnicity, citizenship, and sexuality, and the interactions between them influence our life experiences and opportunities. Those interactions are referred to as intersectionality. What experiences have you had with your own intersectionality (ies)?

3. Family is a theme in *Lone Twin*—the author's mixed family of origin, her first marriage, her uncle's family, and the families that she writes about. How has the author conveyed *differences* in family structures? Do any of the families feel familiar to you? How do you negotiate your life in different families?

4. Second wave feminism focused on women's rights to choose their own destinies. How has the author illustrated, or not, that wave of feminism? Third wave feminism focuses on expanding feminist ideals to all people and the planet, including animals. How has the author embraced, or not, this third wave feminism?

PROJECTS

1. Children and trauma is a recurring theme in *Lone Twin*. How is this theme treated in pop culture? How does the media treat pedophilia?

2. Interview a relative, friend, neighbor or teacher who is from a different generation than you about some memorable day, e.g. 9/11. Ask questions that help the interviewee to locate their personal experience within the public event. Interview another person of that same generation but of a different gender, class, race or ethnicity. Have your interviewees given different accounts? What do you make of those differences?

3. Consider a story in *Lone Twin*. Create an ethnodrama (a dramatic rendition) based on that chapter. Cast it and find an audience!

4. Consider a story in *Lone Twin*. Use its dialogue in a performance piece. Perform it!

CREATIVE WRITING

1. Ask Google for "baby names." Choose a name unfamiliar to you. Write two paragraphs from the point of view of that baby based on your imagination of what a baby with that name would look and be like.

2. Critique your assumptions in 1 (above).

3. Choose a new name. Tell me about yourself.

4. Choose one of Laurel's friends in *Lone Twin*. Tell the story of their

friendship from the friend's point of view. Was she induced into twinning? What did she get from the relationship? How does she feel when the relationship ends?

5. Write the story of your own "twinning" experience, if you had one. Feel free to write about it in the first or third person.

6. Re-write the story in 6 (above) in the voice you did not choose. How has the story changed?

7. Choose one of Laurel's friends in *Lone Twin* and imagine a secret she might have. Write it.

8. Consider writing one of your untold secrets (as Laurel has done in *Lone Twin.*) Consider writing it as "true" as possible, keeping the facts "straight" but using literary devices to express the meaning and feeling of the secret. You don't need to share this but you might ask yourself whether just the writing of it has removed some of the power the secret has held over you.

9. Choose a scene in *Lone Twin* that the author has written in dialogue. Rewrite that scene as exposition. Now, choose a scene that the author has written as exposition and re-write it as dialogue. What have you gained, or lost, by those re-writings?

10. Which person in *Lone Twin* would you like to know more about? Write that person's back-story and put that person in a scene.

11. Several of the scenes in "Cousin Katie" are especially cinematic. Write a screen play for one of those scenes.

12. In *Lone Twin,* the author has changed the names of all non-family members. She has tried to treat everyone respectfully. She wrote a lot of drafts. (As many as fourteen for some stories.) As a draft-writing exercise, choose a real-life situation about which you feel angry or hurt. First, just write it up. Use everyone's real names. Let it rip! Second, change all the identifiers of the persons and places. Calm it down. Third, make everyone you have written about have at least one redeeming feature. Has this method of writing honored your feelings, the feelings of others, and produced a stronger piece of writing?

ABOUT THE AUTHOR

Laurel Richardson is Distinguished Professor Emeritus of Sociology at The Ohio State University where she was also Adjunct Professor of Women's Studies and Adjunct Professor of Cultural Studies. She is an internationally renowned researcher in qualitative methods and arts-based research. She introduced *writing as method of inquiry* into the social sciences and has pioneered writing as poetic representation, ethnodrama, memoir, literary sociology, and critical autoethnography.

Richardson has received multiple awards for her teaching, mentoring, and service for women and minorities, and has been honored in sociology, gender studies, and creative writing. *Permission: The International Interdisciplinary Impact of Laurel Richardson's Work* includes over fifty tributes to her. The International Congress of Qualitative Inquiry (ICQI) honored her with the Lifetime Achievement Award for "dedications and contributions to qualitative research, teaching and practice."

Richardson's work reflects her ethical quest: How can we write to empower others? She has written over two hundred articles and eleven books. Her books on gender, ableism, autoethnography and writing include: *The Dynamics of Sex and Gender* (the first sociology text in the gender studies field)*; Feminist Frontiers* (co-edited anthology, first in field, now in its tenth edition)*; The New Other Woman* (translated into eight languages, most recently into Chinese); *Gender and University Teaching* (co-authored); *Writing Strategies: Reaching Diverse Audiences* (first in its field, still after twenty years); *Travels with Ernest: Crossing the Literary-Ethnographic Divide* (co-authored, first in its field); *Fields of Play: Constructing an Academic Life* (C.H. Cooley Award Winner); *Last Writes: A Daybook for a Dying Friend; After a Fall: A Sociomedical Sojourn* (Honorable Mention/Best Books ICQI); and *Seven Minutes from Home: An American Daughter's Story* (Honorable Mention/Best Books ICQI finalist.)

In addition to her academic accolades, Laurel Richardson has been honored for her poetry, photography, and fiber art, including the cover of this book. She is grateful for friends, family, and colleagues and for all the good things in her life. She lives in Worthington, Ohio with her husband, the novelist Ernest Lockridge, their Papillons—Bashi and Lily—and their sassy black cat, Asia.

Printed in the United States
By Bookmasters